CW00671468

The
Sidmouth
&
Budleigh Salterton
Branches

by
Colin G. Maggs

THE OAKWOOD PRESS

© Oakwood Press and Colin Maggs 1996

British Library Cataloguing in Publication Data
A Record for this book is available from the British Library
ISBN 0 85361 483 0

Typeset by Oakwood Graphics.

Printed by Alpha Print (Oxford) Ltd, Witney, Oxon.

All rights reserved. No part of this book may be reproduced or transmitted in any form or by any means, electronic or mechanical, including photocopying, recording or by any information storage and retrieval system, without permission from the Publisher in writing.

Ex-LSWR 'M7' class 0-4-4T No. 24 is seen with a local train near Budleigh Salterton in June 1934. *E.R. Morten*

Front Cover: The signalman prepares to receive the single line token as BR Standard class '3MT' No. 82013 approaches Sidmouth station with a train from Sidmouth Junction on 13th July, 1960. The other signal arm controls the entrance to the bay platform.
R.C. Riley

Published by
The Oakwood Press
P.O. Box 122, Headington, Oxford

Contents

Chapter One   **History of the Sidmouth Railway** 5

Chapter Two   **Description of the Line to Sidmouth** 19

Chapter Three **Train Services to Sidmouth** 37

Chapter Four   **Locomotives and Coaches on the Sidmouth Branch** 47

Chapter Five   **History of the Budleigh Salterton Railway** 53

Chapter Six   **The Extension from Budleigh Salterton to Exmouth** 61

Chapter Seven **Description of the Line from Tipton St John's**

                     to Exmouth 71

Chapter Eight **Train Services on the Budleigh Salterton Branch** 89

Chapter Nine   **Locomotives and Coaches on the**

                     Budleigh Salterton Branch 99

Appendix   **Station Statistics** 102

                     Bibliography and Acknowledgements 104

BR Standard class '3MT' 2-6-2T No. 82025 having arrived at Budleigh Salterton with a train from Exmouth on 9th July, 1959, has been uncoupled and is running round, ready for the return journey. *R.C. Riley*

The tunnel at the west end of Salcombe Cliffs, Sidmouth, cut for the 1830s line. From the tunnel's mouth, a viaduct spanned the River Sid. *Author*

A period postcard of Church Street, Sidmouth, published in the Frith's Series.

Chapter One

History of the Sidmouth Railway

Sidmouth stands in a valley half a mile wide, through which the small River Sid flows to the sea. The enclosing Peak Hill to the west and Salcombe Hill to the east protect the town from the cold north and east winds and the resort, facing the English Channel, enjoys an equable climate with maximum sunshine. The area occupied by the Romans now lies buried under the shingle which, over many years, has been building up on the seafront. By the beginning of the century the harbour was silting up so that large vessels were unable to come close to shore. As one of Devon's oldest watering places Sidmouth was a famed health resort before 1812, but trade was on the decline, and the inhabitants sought to revive their fortunes by making rail links with the outside world. To some extent they were successful, for the population rose from 3,370 in 1871 to 10,408 in 1951.

In 1811 a scheme for building a harbour at the mouth of the River Sid was defeated, but in 1825 an Act of Parliament was obtained for another harbour project which proved abortive. In 1836 a further Act was passed for a scheme which contemplated enclosing an area of ten acres on the Chit Rocks situated at the west end of the Esplanade, by running out two piers. Large blocks of stone for the construction of these jetties were planned to be brought by rail from Hook Ebb, a reef of rocks exposed at low water and situated 1¾ miles to the east. The railway with a gauge of 3 ft 6 in. to carry the building material ran beside the Esplanade and crossed the River Sid by a small viaduct.

If the line had been built along the foot of Salcombe Hill, it would have run the grave risk of being swept away by waves in a storm, so to prevent this, a tunnel a third of a mile in length was cut through the hill, parallel with the cliff face, and only a few feet from it. One bricked-up entrance to the tunnel about six feet high may still be seen at the west end of Salcombe Hill. At the east end of the tunnel, the line emerged on to shingle and ran along the beach to a stone quay. In the winter of 1966-7 the piles supporting the beach section were exposed. They consisted of tree trunks with their ends pointed and reinforced with metal so that they could be driven into rock.

A blacksmith named Coles was commissioned to construct a machine to run on rails with which to transport the blocks along the railway, but since it was only worked by foot power, it lacked sufficient drive and an alternative had to be sought, and so a steam locomotive was ordered. It was delivered by sea, and the weather being fine, the vessel carrying it was run on to the beach. They then discovered that no crane was available for unloading such a weight, so the ship was floated off on the tide and sent to Exmouth where a sufficiently strong crane was available to offload the locomotive. This was then drawn by horses over the hilly roads to Sidmouth, which it entered decorated with laurels. The engine was placed on the rails opposite the Esplanade and run to the mouth of the tunnel, which, to the chagrin of all concerned, it was found to be too large to enter. In order not to waste such a curiosity, it was coupled to some wagons and for a small fee the inhabitants were drawn backwards and forwards along the Esplanade for pure entertainment.

By 1838 the locomotive was removed, the piles of the viaduct across the Sid sawn off, and the mouth of the tunnel walled up as it proved too handy for the concealment of smuggled kegs of brandy. Although the foundation stone of the harbour had been laid on Chit Rocks with great ceremony, no further work was carried out. Of the estimated £15,000 cost of the project, nearly £12,000 had actually been spent and was a complete loss to the investors.

In 1846 the proposed Exeter, Yeovil & Dorchester Railway planned a branch to Sidmouth, but the whole project proved abortive. In 1852 the 'broad gauge' party put forward a similar unsuccessful scheme: the Devon & Dorset Railway jointly promoted by the Great Western Railway and the Bristol & Exeter Railway, and intended to run from Maiden Newton to Exeter, with a branch running to Sidmouth.

In 1853 the inhabitants discussed the Central Western Railway, a direct route to London, badly needed as the existing circuitous route was by road to Exeter and then onwards by rail via Bristol and Swindon. The Central Western Railway became the Salisbury & Yeovil Railway, which was opened to Exeter on 18th July, 1860, and whose station at Feniton was only about nine miles from Sidmouth.

Londoners convened a meeting at Sidmouth on 18th December, 1861 for the purpose of planning a railway to run from Sidmouth to Feniton and combining it with a harbour scheme. The Sidmouth & Harbour Co. received its Act of Parliament, 25 & 26 Vic. cap. 227, on 7th August, 1862 and this authorised the raising of capital of £120,000 and £40,000 on loan. £90,000 was applicable to the railway only. The London & South Western Railway was authorised to lease the line in perpetuity for an annual rental of £5,000. The scheme proved to be unpopular with subscribers and money was slow to come in.

In 1864 Shrimpton, who had taken the railway part of the contract, was forced to abandon the work as he had not received any plans. It was also discovered that shareholders had been divided into two classes: Class A which included Sidmouth residents and Class B which comprised those in London. Calls for money were only made on Class A. Angry shareholders held a meeting at the Royal York Hotel, Sidmouth on 8th November, 1864 when their resolution condemned the Engineer H.H. Bird, as the principal, if not sole, cause of the slowness of the work.

On 5th July, 1865 an Act 28 & 29 Vic. cap. 237 authorised the company to construct a half-mile-long line at Sidmouth, for which no new capital was to be raised. At a meeting on 30th November, 1866 it was found that the liabilities of the company amounted to £20,000, nearly £16,000 of which was due to Shrimpton. Sidmouth shareholders refused to pay their calls, but threatened with prosecution, agreed to pay half within a week and the rest before 15th January, 1867. However, the company expired in 1869.

Meanwhile the trustees of the Balfour family, who had purchased the manor of Sidmouth, decided to promote a Bill and this received Royal Assent on 29th June, 1871 (34 & 35 Vic. cap. 68), authorising a capital of £66,000, and borrowing powers of £22,000. It proved to be a bona fide project, and the work of constructing the line went ahead. The company's Directors were Sir John Kennaway MP (Chairman); John Fulford Vicary of North Tawton; John Macmillan Dunlop of Windermere; Neil Bannatyne and John Heugh of London.

An article of agreement between the provisional Directors of the Sidmouth Railway and the LSWR, dated the 17th March, 1871 and confirmed by the Act, stated that the line could be constructed as a light railway according to the Regulations of Railways Act, 1868. It said that no station was to be on a steeper gradient than 1 in 300 and went on to stipulate that stations 'shall also include proper and sufficient station and gate houses, working-sheds, station yards and approaches, station buildings and accommodation, goods sheds, engine sheds, carriage sheds, sidings, turntables, water cranes, tanks and water, loading, cranes and other works and conveniences such as in all respects the owning Company would have to construct if they had been about to work the Railway'. The agreement continued by ruling that no structures were to be of timber, and the Vignoles rails must not weigh less than 60 lb./yd. The Sidmouth company was to maintain the line for one year from opening and the LSWR would work it for 55 per cent when gross earnings did not exceed £4,000, and 50 per cent when above that figure. The LSWR had the option to purchase the railway. This line received local support and its shares were taken up.

At the Board meeting held on 5th July, 1872 the tender of R.T. Relf, Okehampton was accepted for £35,000, he agreeing to forfeit a hundred pounds for every week after 31st July, 1874 that the railway remained incomplete. Later, Relf found he had tendered too low a price for the erection of the three stations and begged for an additional £7,000. The dispute arose because at the time the contract was signed, the stations were not designed, but the company stated that they could be built for £7,000 and on this understanding Relf entered the work. However, when the designs were eventually furnished, he found they would cost a minimum of £17,000, and cause him considerable loss.

The Directors compromised by offering £2,000 on condition that the line was opened for traffic by 30th June. The total additional cost to the contractor proved to be £9,000, and although the line was opened a week late on 6th July, 1874, the Directors still granted him the £2,000. Suing for the balance, Relf's counsel declared he was £7,000 out of pocket by the construction of the line, but in July 1875 after the judge had examined the case, he regretted to say that the plaintiff had made himself liable and so was non-suited.

The line being finished, Colonel F.H. Rich carried out the Board of Trade Inspection and made the following report:

The Secretary,   2nd July 1874
Board of Trade

Sir,

I have the honour to report for the information of the Board of Trade in compliance with the Instructions contained in your Minute of the 25th ultimo, I have inspected the Sidmouth Railway.

It extends from Sidmouth to Ottery Road on the London and South Western Railway. There is no Junction at Ottery Road for Passenger Trains as they are intended to run into a Dock line at the back of the present Platform.

'02' class 0-4-4T No. 182 arrives at Ottery St Mary with a down train of 10 coaches, *c.* 1910. Four uniformed staff can be seen. *Lens of Sutton*

An '02' class 0-4-4T enters Ottery St Mary with an up 4-coach train, *c.* 1910; notice the brick-built waiting shelter on the up platform. *Author's Collection*

The new line is to be worked by the London and South Western Railway Company.

The Sidmouth Railway is about 8¼ miles long - It is a single Line with loop lines and sidings at the Stations - Land has been purchased for a double line.

The gauge is 4 feet 8½ inches.

The Permanent Way consists of a Vignoles Pattern rail that weighs 60 to 62 lbs per lineal yard. It is fished and fixed with fang bolts and spikes to transverse Sleepers laid 3 feet apart except those next to the rail joints which are only 2 feet apart.

The line is well-ballasted with broken stone and gravel.

The Stations are Ottery St Mary, Tipton and Sidmouth.

There are turntables at Sidmouth and Ottery Road.

The works consist of 7 over, 7 under bridges and 2 Viaducts which are constructed of brick and stone. The widest span is 44 feet on the Skew. These works appear to be substantially constructed.

There are 4 authorized Level Crossings at public Roads which are provided with Gates to close across the Road and Railway and are interlocked with the signals.

The following points require to be attended to:

The Gates across the public Roads require stops to prevent their being opened so as to allow a free passage both along the Railway and the public Road.

The locking of one Siding at Ottery Road requires to be completed so that the Railway Signals can only be lowered for one direction at a time.

Two blind sidings or catch points are required for the sidings at the West Side of the line at Sidmouth Station and two facing points, bolts and locks on the facing points at the entrance of the Station. The starting Signals at Sidmouth should be moved to the North Side of the Junction Cabin and Spring buffers should be provided for the Dock lines.

The Engineer has promised to have these matters attended to at once and I submit that the Board of Trade may sanction the opening of the Sidmouth Railway.

I enclose an undertaking as to the mode proposed for working this Single Line which is satisfactory.

Yours etc.
Signed F.H. Rich
Colonel R.E.

P.S. There are deviations vertically beyond the Limits allowed, from 5 miles 11 chains to 6 miles 70 chains but I am informed that the Land Owners have raised no objections to these deviations and the gradients of the Railway have not been altered thereby.

The ballast had been delivered by 'Ilfracombe Goods' 0-6-0s Nos. 282, 283 and 284, new locomotives which were on loan to the Engineer's Department until the line for which they were intended were opened.

The first train left Sidmouth Junction at 6.50 am on Monday 6th July, 1874. Fares were fixed at: Exeter to Sidmouth single, First class 4s. 0d.; Second class 2s. 6d.; Third class 1s. 8d. There was no official opening that day, but 200 people gathered to see the initial train leave. Rather unusually, celebrations were spread out over no less than four days. On 6th July, 800 children marched behind a band from the Esplanade to Sidmouth station to watch the departure of the 2.45 pm and cheered 'loudly and long'. They adjourned to a nearby field in Landpart for tea and games and 'loads of nic-nacs and useful articles' were distributed. The cost of these junketings was £44 18s. 8½d. Tipton and Ottery also celebrated the occasion by holding teas for young and old.

A view at Tipton St Johns looking 'up', *c.* 1905. There are water columns at the ends of the platforms, the vertical pipe of which is enshrouded in a wooden casing to prevent freezing. On the down platform is a brick-built waiting shelter with a ground frame hut beyond. There are five uniformed staff to be seen. An additional notice under the station name board reads: 'Change for East Budleigh, Budleigh Salterton & Exmouth'. *Lens of Sutton*

Tipton St John's level crossing, *c.* 1920. The right hand window to the locking room of the signal box has yet to be blocked up. *Author's Collection*

The following day 'a first class dinner' at Sidmouth Town Hall was given by the Manor Trustees when about 60 of the railway shareholders, officials, gentry and tradesman attended. The 8th July was regatta day, and because of the existence of the railway, more people came to Sidmouth than ever before, one special train of 17 coaches being double-headed. The editor of *Lethaby's Sidmouth Journal & Directory* wrote in the leading article of the August issue: 'There was a seeming incongruity in linking the railway opening with a waterside rollicking; and in providing an amusement which is proverbial for bringing together all the rowdyism of the district . . . giving knaves a welcome and thereby attracting the fools on whom such knaves flourish'. Select Sidmouth was experiencing just the sort of behaviour it feared would occur when the railway was opened.

On Thursday there were railway trips, a public dinner for 400 old people in the Knowle Grounds and a distribution of sixpence to old people under seventy, 145 coins being issued, and a shilling to everyone over that age (238). Eighty-one 'very aged and infirm' folk unable to come received half a crown each, while 84 lb. of surplus meat and 24 lb. of plum pudding was divided among thirty families. Altogether 464 people were entertained and a hundred of these were treated to a trip on the railway.

Contrasting with the events recorded the previous month, September 1874 saw the *Sidmouth Journal & Directory* reporting the line's 'astonishing success' in bringing hundreds of orderly strangers to the town, whose 'streets and esplanade have presented appearances such as had not been witnessed by the oldest inhabitants'. The *Western Gazette* acclaimed Sidmouth to be 'a new watering place' extolling its low prices, narrow but clean streets and its inhabitants who were 'a very quiet and orderly set of people' without the 'characteristic vices' of larger resorts, and whose 'boatmen don't swear much'.

On 1st October, 1912 W.H. Hastings, Secretary of the Sidmouth Railway and also a director of the Sidmouth Hotels Co. Limited and Sidmouth Baths, wrote to H.A. Walker who had been appointed General Manager to the LSWR on 1st January that year. Hastings observed that train fares earned by the main line from Victoria Hotel guests amounted to £4,000 a year. This revenue came from London businessmen coming down for the weekends, while their families stayed at the hotel. Hastings pressed for through coaches to be run from Liverpool and Manchester, Leeds and Bradford, via the Midland Railway, Somerset & Dorset Joint Railway and the LSWR:

Through carriages leaving the North Country termini would not act merely as an advertisement for the places on your system, but they would also induce people to select *your* places on account of convenience of travelling; but at present your system is suffering from the fact that whereas through carriages come from Glasgow, Liverpool, Manchester and other Northern places via North Western and Great Western to Exeter and Plymouth, there is no corresponding through service on the South Western Railway. This gives Torquay, Teignmouth, and other watering places on the Great Western Railway a very great advantage over the South Western Company's places. You told me, I remember, that there might be great difficulty in arranging for through carriages from Liverpool and Manchester on account of the existence of an agreement between the Great Western and North Western. The Midland however, also taps Manchester and Liverpool and possibly something may be done in that direction.

Looking towards the stop blocks at Sidmouth, *c.* 1910. Run-round loop in foreground, white-painted lever, *left*.   *Author's Collection*

An '02' class 0-4-4T enters Sidmouth with a 6-coach train from Sidmouth Junction, *c.* 1910. Note the 'barley sugar' pattern lampposts on the platform; the signal box at the far end of the layout; the creeper-covered goods shed, *centre right*; and the porters' barrow labelled 'Sidmouth'.
Author's Collection

Hastings told Walker that shortly before Sir Charles J. Owens retired as General Manager of the LSWR on 31st December, 1911, that he, Hastings, heard

> . . . . a good many comments from travellers which do not reach your ears, and I can assure you that it is no uncommon remark that passengers say they will not come to the East Devon places again, but will go to Teignmouth, Dawlish, Torquay, etc., in preference on future occasions on account of the inconvenient journey to the East Devon places.
>
> It has become so serious, and we are conscious of losing so much business in this way that with a view of retaining that North-Country connection which we have already gained, and of increasing it, unless something is done on the part of the South Western Railway to assist us, you may, I think, expect that the Hotels here will continue with a good Motor Service between St David's (GWR station) Exeter and Sidmouth and will advertise this service extensively in the North.

He went on to point out that it was in winter and spring, rather than summer, that people came from the North to stay at Sidmouth, and would come in greater numbers if there was a better service.

In reply, Walker said that he believed that many passengers from the North would always want to travel to the West of England via London. It is likely that Walker's view was coloured by the fact that the LSWR benefitted by receipts from a greater mileage over its tracks than if they travelled cross-country.

Hastings pointed out in his reply of 7th February, 1913:

> The danger, however, seems to me to be that a large number of people who consider matters of expense will prefer to go by the direct route to the GWR Company's watering-places because of the through-carriages and more moderate cost of going through; that is to say without disturbing what is already coming to the South-Western watering-places there is, to my certain knowledge, a lot of business going past your system of which we might get a share. You have a sea-board here in East Devon which given a fair chance, may easily grow as important to your system as Bournemouth.

As no through coaches from the North were put on, the correspondence continued into 1914 when on 29th May Hastings wrote: 'The main line trains on the South Western and Great Western do not correspond very well [at Exeter] probably because it does not suit the South Western to increase facilities for East Devon people to make use of the Great Western trains from London and the North. It would however, be an advantage to Sidmouth if a better correspondence existed.'

Hastings' suggestion was never adopted but the LSWR certainly recognised Sidmouth's importance and following the Armistice in 1918, purchased the Knowle Hotel near the golf links.

In 1914 tourist ticket rates from Waterloo to Sidmouth were: First class £2 8s. 6d.; Second class £1 10s. 6d.; Third class £1 6s. 3d. In comparison, by May 1966 fares for ordinary returns were: First class £6 16s. 6d.; Second class £4 11s. 0d.

During World War I the company's Chairman Colonel J.E.H. Balfour, was fighting with the British Expeditionary Force in France and on 16th July, 1917 was sent a letter:

A 'T1' class 0-4-4T locomotive stands outside the locomotive shed, *c.* 1905. The goods shed can
be seen on the far left. *Lens of Sutton*

A 'T1' class 0-4-4T, No. 14, stands at Sidmouth in the 1920s. *Miss Freda Clayton*

Dear Sir

The Board & General Meeting of this Company must be held in the early part of next month. Will you be good enough to name a date and inform me whether you will be able to attend and preside?
Of the 5 Directors, 2 are with the Army and 1 is in a nursing home, lately returned sick from Mesopotamia.
There are only 2 available in England - and it needs 3 to make a quorum.

I am
Yours truly
W.H. Hastings
Secy.

Balfour was able to be granted leave and returned home for the meeting.

Despite the lack of through coaches, the Sidmouth Railway Company flourished and remained financially independent - this was unusual as small companies were generally soon taken over by a larger concern. In 1894 the LSWR had attempted to purchase the line for £70,050 cash, but no mutual agreement could be reached and it continued independent until 1922. A special general meeting was held at the company's registered general office, Sidmouth, on 15th November that year to consider the Scheme of Absorption which was explained by the Sidmouth Railway's Secretary and Solicitor W.H. Hastings. 'The London & South Western Railway (Southern Group) Preliminary Absorption Group 1922' was approved so far as it related to the Sidmouth Railway. The company's ordinary stock was exchanged for LSWR debentures and preference shares. On 1st January, 1948 the line became part of British Railways, Southern Region, things continuing much as before until 1st January, 1963 when the regional boundaries were re-drawn and the branch transferred to the Western Region.

In the 1963 Beeching Report the line was threatened with closure, and organisations such as hoteliers and shopkeepers interested in keeping the line open, formed the Sidmouth Railway Committee, about 120 people attending the inaugural meeting. They considered the railway most important, as Sidmouth as a town had deliberately chosen to be a select holiday resort, catering for the particular type of person who looked for peace, quiet and natural charm. Sidmouth's economic survival being largely dependent on its holiday trade, it was very vulnerable to change in holiday habits. They were afraid that any reduction in the number of holiday-makers as a result of the closure of the line, would remove the margin on which the economy of the town depended. If hotels and boarding houses lost money, it would be reflected in loss of trade to the shops. The Sidmouth Railway Committee set up with representatives of the Chamber of Trade, the Hoteliers, the Sid Vale Associations, Ratepayers' Association and backed by Sidmouth Urban District Council, planned to fight closure and improve rail facilities to Sidmouth. One of the committee's achievements was that from 6th January, 1964, seat reservations bookable at Sidmouth, would be made available for passengers joining the 10.30 am Exeter-Waterloo at Sidmouth Junction, this facility replacing the through coaches from Sidmouth.

British Railways regretted that it could find no economic way of providing a fast through diesel service from Sidmouth to Exeter, as, to pay their way, trains

'M7' class 0-4-4T No. 30676 stands at Ottery St Mary with through coaches from the down 'Atlantic Coast Express', 4th September, 1958.   *H.B. Priestley*

'M7' class 0-4-4T No. 30024 leaves Sidmouth with the 4.30 pm to Sidmouth Junction, 16th August, 1960.   *H.B. Priestley*

had to stop at all stations. However the branch was 'dieselised' in November 1963 and it was hoped by this means to reduce the deficit on one hand, and increase the patronage of the service on the other. Because of the diesel service, in 1964 through coaches to and from Waterloo were only provided on summer Saturdays, this facility continuing until the end of the summer 1965. However, with the withdrawal of the daily through coach, quite a few people wishing to travel to London went by car or taxi to the main line station at Axminster.

Sidmouth admitted that the town had derived a great deal of its prosperity from the excellent rail service. In 1964 a fair proportion of visitors still found rail the most satisfactory means of travel and the committee wished to determine what effect closure of the line would have on the prosperity of the town. To this end a census was carried out. The Hotels & Caterers Association ascertained that 20 per cent of holiday makers travelled to Sidmouth by rail, a considerable number stating that they would not holiday at Sidmouth if no such facilities were available. About five per cent of visitors to large hotels came by rail, but smaller boarding houses had a higher percentage, in some cases 50 per cent, giving a total average of 20 per cent. On a summer Saturday, 900 passengers used Sidmouth station, while 30 to 40 used it daily in winter, the number increasing to over a 100 in summer. Each year, 175,000 passengers used the station while Tipton and Ottery St Mary together accounted for another 115,000.

Closure was protracted. A letter from the Ministry of Transport dated 22nd December, 1965 said that it would ensure good bus/rail connections at Honiton and that porterage staff would assist in bus/rail transfer. Closure would not take place before October 1966 and even then not until additional bus services had been authorised by road service licence. In February 1967 it was announced that the Devon General bus company would operate extra bus services from Exmouth-Tipton St John's; Sidmouth-Honiton via Tipton St John's and Ottery St Mary; Whimple-Ottery St Mary and Whimple-Honiton. Although at first the replacement bus services were lavish, linking at Honiton even with trains that had had no previous rail connecting service, by 1976 they had diminished to one bus each way daily connecting in and out of 3.00 pm Waterloo and 5.55 pm Exeter at Honiton, plus one other bus which did not connect with anything effectively. Both these were Exeter-Honiton services with Sidmouth connections at Ottery St Mary.

The last passenger train to run on the line was the 6.57 pm Sidmouth Junction-Sidmouth on 4th March, 1967. Tipton was the West Country's last junction between two single line branches, and even at closure was served by almost 30 trains daily. It had been closed to goods on 27th January, 1964, Sidmouth Junction, Ottery St Mary and Sidmouth following on 6th September, 1965. The last two remained open as coal depots until 8th May, 1967. Connection with the main line at Sidmouth Junction was severed when it was singled on 11th June, 1967, compelling track-lifting trains to work via Exmouth. On 10th July, 1968, severe floods breached the Budleigh Salterton line at Newton Poppleford and East Budleigh, leaving two isolated stretches of track: East Budleigh-Ottery St Mary and Tipton St John's-Sidmouth and marooning a train of wagons at Tipton. The remaining sections of track and rolling stock were perforce removed by road. Closure of Sidmouth Junction was not the end of that station, for on 3rd May, 1971 it was re-opened as Feniton, catering for morning and evening commuter traffic.

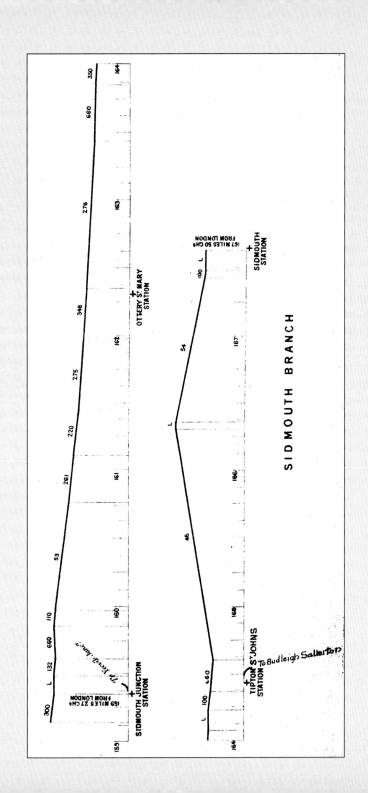

SIDMOUTH BRANCH

Chapter Two

Description of the Line to Sidmouth

Sidmouth Junction was a two-platform station 159 miles 22 chains from Waterloo. It experienced an exceptional number of name changes. Opened as Feniton on 18th July 1860, it became Ottery & Sidmouth Road 1st July, 1861; Feniton for Ottery St Mary, February 1868; Ottery Road, April 1868; Sidmouth Junction, 6th July, 1874 and as mentioned above, reverted to Feniton when re-opened on 3rd May, 1971.

Sidmouth trains used the bay at the east end of the down platform, trains entering it facing Exeter. No engine release road was provided and the engine had to back the train out of the bay platform in order to run round, but was able to perform the entire manoeuvre without fouling the main line. The tall LSWR signal box was situated a short distance from the station and a member of the platform staff was responsible for fetching or surrendering the single line tablet lowered on a rope. The goods shed was placed near the down platform, and a turntable, removed about 1930, was sited at the east end of the goods yard, the sidings in the yard being taken out of use on 8th May, 1967. All but one of these were on the down side, the solitary siding on the up side being one of considerable length used by goods trains awaiting a path up Honiton Bank. Unlike Seaton Junction, the station was not modernised, retaining its two low short platforms until the end. The down platform by virtue of being placed between the level crossing gates at the Exeter end and the goods yard at the other, was short and necessitated trains of any reasonable length having to pull forward and draw up again. For re-opening, when housing development in the area gave a greater potential traffic, mainly commuters between Feniton and Exeter, a portable building was placed on part of what was the former down platform. A nearby row of railwaymen's cottages was colloquially known as 'Rat's Castle'.

On leaving the station, the branch line, after descending a gradient of 1 in 110 soon steepening to 1 in 53, had for the most part easy gradients along the valley of the River Otter towards Ottery St Mary. The heaviest cutting, half a mile in length, was entered soon after leaving the junction. Gosford Gates crossing, approximately midway between the junction and Ottery St Mary, had a 5-lever Westinghouse frame comprising: gate lock, up distant, up home, down home, and down distant levers. The lodge is still occupied and one of the former crossing gates is now an entrance to a field.

Cadhay Gates, half a mile further on, had a similar frame and was manned in later years by a female crossing keeper. Arrangements were made to supply coal and stores to these two crossings: Gosford Gates was serviced by the 9.10 am freight from the Junction and Cadhay Gates by a porter from Ottery St Mary. In later years a light engine or freight train picked up empty churns, or set down full water churns at Cadhay Gates.

Ottery St Mary(162 m. 14 ch.), was a typical country station with crossing loop, three sidings and goods shed. The loop was extended southwards for 2

'M7' class 0-4-4T No. 671 stands in the bay platform at Sidmouth Jn in May 1935, with a train for the branch. *L.T. Catchpole*

'Merchant Navy' class 4-6-2 No. 35025 *Brocklebank Line* with the 8.10 am Ilfracombe to Waterloo, picks up the through coaches from the 9.52 am Exmouth/10.20 am Sidmouth at Sidmouth Jn. Class '2MT' 2-6-2T No. 41318, shedded at 72A (Exmouth Junction), stands in the down bay platform heading a branch train, 31st May, 1963. *J.H. Aston*

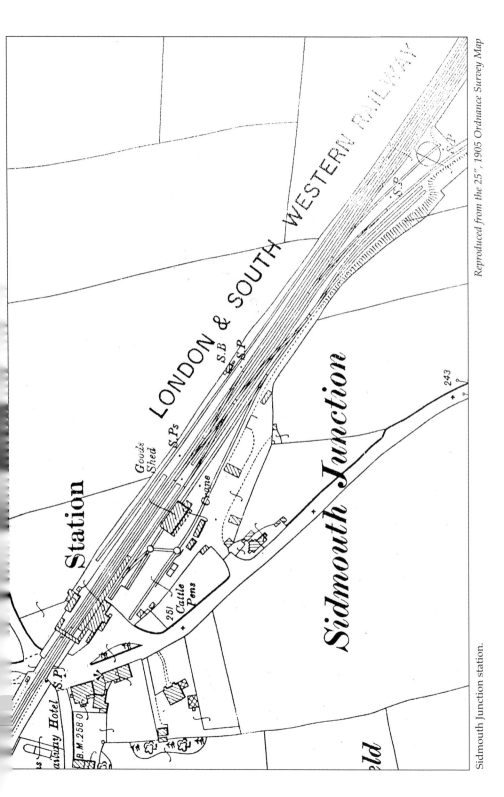

Reproduced from the 25", 1905 Ordnance Survey Map

Sidmouth Junction station.

'Warship' class diesel-hydraulic No. D827 *Kelly* leaves Sidmouth Jn with the 2.10 pm Exeter St David's to Waterloo, while the 2-car dmu forming the 2.55 pm to Sidmouth stands in the bay, 25th February, 1967. *R.A. Lumber*

A close-up of the comprehensive name board at the west end of the up platform. *Lens of Sutton*

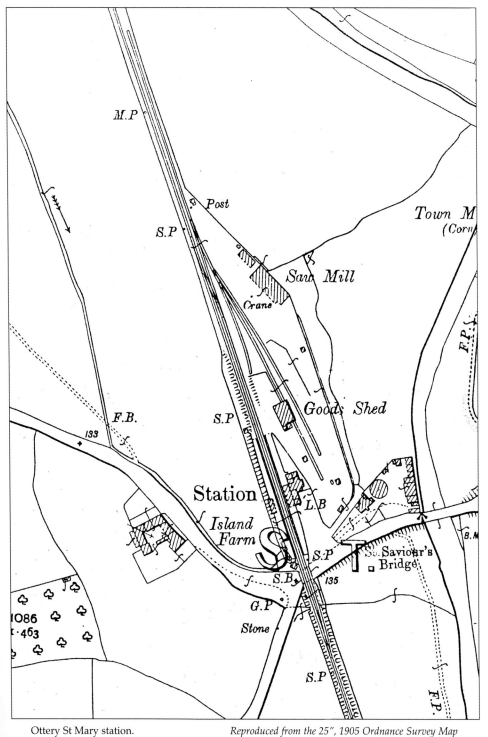

Ottery St Mary station.

Reproduced from the 25", 1905 Ordnance Survey Map

The 4.40 pm Sidmouth Junction to Sidmouth comprising a 2-car dmu, leaves Ottery St Mary on 4th March, 1967, the last day of passenger working. *R.A. Lumber*

The up direction view at Ottery St Mary showing the 1955-built signal box. The signal post consists of two rails bolted together. *Lens of Sutton*

A view showing the waiting shelter on the up platform. The goods yard is on the right beyond the end of the platforms.
Lens of Sutton

The original, low, timber-built signal box at Ottery St Mary; view towards Sidmouth Junction, 30th May, 1936.
S.W. Baker

This view in the down direction is dated *c*. 1905; the ground frame hut is on the left.

Courtesy: Railway Magazine

A view in the down direction taken after modification of the junction at Tipton St John's in 1954. The water tower stands beyond the footbridge. An enamel notice under the canopy of the up platform reads: 'This platform for Sidmouth Junction. Over the bridge for Sidmouth Town and Exmouth line'. (Sidmouth was not normally referred to as 'Sidmouth Town'.) The level crossing gates are just being closed to road traffic to allow an approaching train from Budleigh Salterton to pass. *Lens of Sutton*

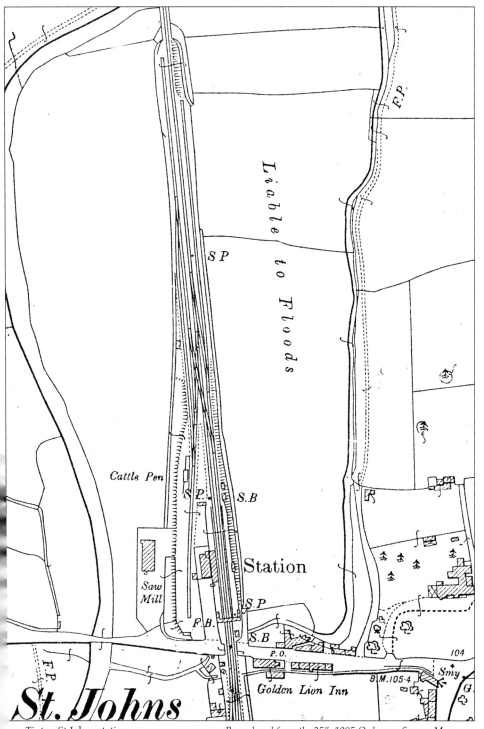

Tipton St Johns station.   *Reproduced from the 25″, 1905 Ordnance Survey Map*

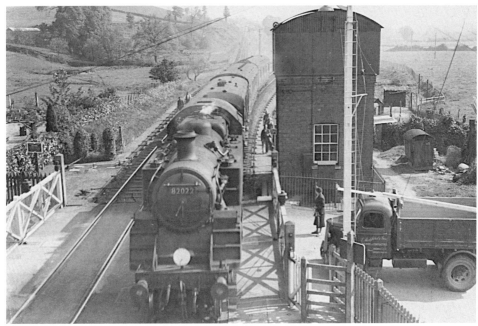

BR Standard class '3MT' 2-6-2T No. 82022 enters Tipton St John's from Exmouth in the 1950s. The Sidmouth line ascends at 1 in 45 behind the second coach.   *P.Q. Treloar*

View of the junction at Tipton St John's, looking north from the Harpford Lane overbridge, *c.* 1910.   *Author's Collection*

chains on 22nd November, 1936. Like all the stations on the branch, the two-storey gabled brick station house was built of brick as was the waiting shelter on the opposite platform. The platform canopy was supported by decorative cast iron brackets. The former station is now a Resource Centre with a rather lurid mural on an outside wall. The brick goods shed had a lean-to office. The signal box on the up side at the south end of the station controlled the level crossing. During World War II this box was operated by a signalwoman. On 20th November, 1955 the structure was replaced by a new box on the opposite side of the track.

About 1946 the booking clerk at Ottery St Mary was replaced by a leading porter. Among the traffic despatched were boxes of mushrooms for Covent Garden, while day-old chicks were sent off each Friday, hatching day, leaving in passenger train brake vans. Ottery St Mary Market was held on alternate Mondays and, if the number of cattle trucks was too great to be hauled by the scheduled goods train, a 4.20 pm cattle special ran from Ottery St Mary to Sidmouth Junction where the vans were shunted on to various main line trains. A cattle special was hauled by a tender engine, either a '700' class 0-6-0 'Black Motor', or an 'A12' class 'Jubilee', as a tank engine was likely to run out of water and no column was sited at Ottery St Mary for replenishment. At 164 m. 05 ch., the 55 yards long Ottery St Mary viaduct spanned the River Otter.

Tipton St John's, (164 m. 24 ch.), just 'Tipton' until 1st February, 1881, was a busy two-platform station immediately north of the junction of the Exmouth and Sidmouth branches and a locomotive watering point. On weekdays it dealt with two- to three- coach trains, timetables usually arranging for an up train from Sidmouth and another from Exmouth, to approach Tipton St John's within a few minutes of each other. The first train terminated and the second proceeded to Sidmouth Junction. The terminating train having been emptied, drew forward to the up sidings where a loop enabled its locomotive to run-round without fouling the main line. Up and down trains passed, after which the train in the up sidings drew forward and crossed to the down platform to form a connecting service for whichever line had not been served by the preceding down train. On summer Saturdays there were eleven-coach trains to be divided and joined.

The original signal box was on the Sidmouth side of the level crossing, but in March 1897, preparing for the Budleigh Salterton Railway, a new box was opened diagonally over the crossing at the end of the down platform. It was equipped with 32 levers, while in addition a 4-lever ground frame at the up end of the station worked some points and facing point locks. This ground frame was taken out of use on 23rd February, 1930, from which date all points were operated from the signal box (rated Class 3 - as high as many main line boxes).

When first opened Tipton had been the least important station on the branch and had only one siding, but the opening of the Budleigh line turned it into an important junction. When the new box and additional sidings were inspected by the Board of Trade officer on 17th April, 1897, he expressed concern regarding the risk to passengers passing over the line by means of a sleeper crossing and recommended that a footbridge be provided, this being completed by the following February. The lengths of the up and down platforms were 250

Class '2MT' 2-6-2T No. 41323 (shedded 72A Exmouth Junction), climbs near Bowd with the 10.28 am Sidmouth Junction to Sidmouth, 24th August, 1963. *Author*

Class 'M7' 0-4-4T No. 30323 passes under the then B3176 road overbridge, with the 4.5 pm train from Sidmouth on the approach to Harpford Wood at Bowd, some 1⅜ miles from Sidmouth, 21st August, 1955. *E.R. Morten*

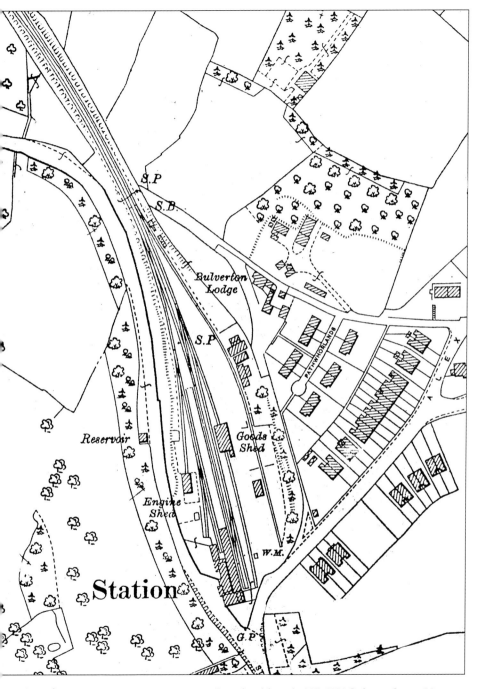

Sidmouth station.

Reproduced from the 25″, 1934 Ordnance Survey Map

A view of the signal box and yard at Sidmouth, 13th July, 1960. The siding to J.P. White's motor caravan works runs behind the signal box. The coal siding is to the left of the Ford Popular, while on the far right is the end of the goods shed. *R.C. Riley*

A view of the former engine shed at Sidmouth in July 1960 about 30 years after closure. The coach on the left bears the Eastern Region No. E15722. This was a Mark I 'CK' (composite corridor). *R.C. Riley*

General view towards the buffer stops at Sidmouth. The headcode on the tank engine heading the passenger train indicates that it is bound for Exmouth. Note the engine pit, *right*, with adjacent piles of ashes.

Lens of Sutton

A more recent view of the same location. The track has been cut short of the locomotive shed which has been converted to other use. Note the gas lamp, *left*, illuminating the enamel name board which has replaced the concrete one depicted in an earlier view. The lamp standard of 'barley sugar' pattern beyond, has had a neck added to give the gas lamp greater height.

Lens of Sutton

The Railway Station, Sidmouth.

The exterior of Sidmouth station *c.* 1905, showing a variety of horse-drawn vehicles. The rear of the engine shed is to the left of centre. The creeper-covered house to the right is the station master's. *Author's Collection*

An exterior view of Sidmouth station, *c.* 1965. *Lens of Sutton*

and 244 feet respectively. Camping coaches were stabled in one of the three sidings: in 1955 a six-berth coach was let at a rental of £9 per week in the high season. The single storey station is now a private house.

The actual junction, formerly double track becoming single beyond, was altered on 28th February, 1954 making the Sidmouth branch junction single.

From Tipton the Sidmouth branch rose very impressively at 1 in 45 for two miles to Bowd Summit in Harpford Woods and then fell for about a mile at 1 in 54 to the terminus (167 m. 39 ch.), situated high on a hill above the town, 200 ft above sea level and some ¾ mile from the beach. It is said that it was built inland purposely to discourage trippers spoiling the select town.

The station entrance had a wooden valanced canopy above two semi-circular arched doorways, the windows having limestone lintels and sills and the gables decorative finial spikes. The platform canopy was supported by decorative cast-iron brackets. At the terminal end of the platform was a substantial gabled, red-brick station house, with yellow-brick dressings. The platform held seven coaches on its east face and five on the west face. This limited accommodation set problems on occasions such as when the 'City of Plymouth Holiday Express' arrived with nine coaches behind a 'West Country' class Pacific. Another engine had to divide the train between platforms. To release an engine arriving on the road serving the western platform face, the train was backed into a siding, the locomotive shunted out of the way and the train run back to the platform by gravity.

There was a large goods shed, engine shed and turntable. The engine shed was closed and the turntable removed in the 1930s. The tall signal box had a 23-lever frame. A private siding ran to Sidmouth gas works. The station building is now used by J.H. Dunsford & Sons Ltd, builders, the station yard for light engineering and the station house is now a private residence.

A horse-drawn bus ran to and from the station. For a charge of sixpence per passenger, it would call at his home and convey him to the station, or from the station to his house.

Sidmouth station, viewed from the buffer stops. The run-round loop is on the right.
Lens of Sutton

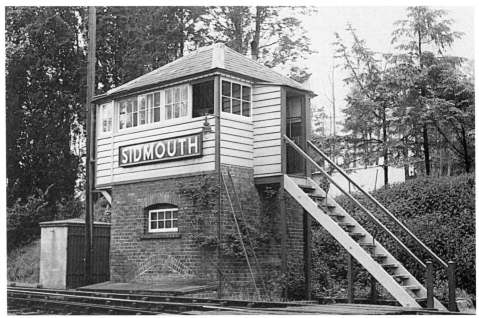

Sidmouth signal box on 29th May, 1963; notice the metal ladder to give access to the gas lamp. A house-proud signalman has left a scrubbing brush on the stair stringer between the third and fourth steps from the top. *J.H. Aston*

BR Standard class '3MT' 2-6-2T No. 82011 pulls into the platform at Sidmouth with the 1.00 pm from Sidmouth Junction on 4th September, 1958. *H.B. Priestley*

Chapter Three

Train Services to Sidmouth

When the branch opened in 1874, seven passenger trains ran each way daily taking 28-30 minutes in each direction. No Sunday service was run and all trains had first, second and third class accommodation. In November 1874 the early morning return trip was abolished, reducing the number of trains to six each way. As the engine was stabled overnight at Sidmouth, the first train started from that resort and the last train terminated there. In August 1887, seven trains ran each way on weekdays only, one down train taking only 25 minutes. For the period 1st October, 1903-31st May, 1904, eight down passenger trains were run, plus one mixed train; there was one separate goods train and a path allowed for a conditional goods. In the up direction were nine passenger trains, one goods and one conditional goods. From 1st June-30th September, 1909 the service was:- Down: 10 passenger; 1 mixed; 1 mixed Tipton-Sidmouth; 1 goods. Up: 11 passenger; 1 goods. From 7th June to 30th September 1914, eleven passenger trains ran each way, some doing the journey in 23 minutes, one goods train being run in each direction. There was also one down mixed train.

The 1938 summer timetable showed 24 trains each way on Mondays-Fridays, operating over all or part of the branch. These consisted of 11 passenger trains each way between Sidmouth Junction and Sidmouth, two between Ottery St Mary and Exmouth, two Sidmouth Junction and Exmouth; five Tipton St John's and Sidmouth, three of which were through to or from Exmouth, and an odd working from Tipton St John's to Ottery St Mary and back. The remainder were freight workings; the 7.00 am from Sidmouth Junction to Sidmouth; 7.45 am Exmouth Junction-Exmouth via the branch, this latter train returning first at 10.46 am and the former at 2.35 pm. The Exmouth passenger workings had connecting trains between Tipton St John's and Sidmouth. Three passenger trains each way were through to or from Exeter Central (5.50, 7.34, 8.00 am from Exeter, 10.20 am, 3.15, 10.25 pm from Sidmouth).

On Saturdays in 1938 there were 30 down and 28 up workings. These consisted of 16 down, 15 up between Sidmouth Junction and Sidmouth; 2 between Ottery St Mary and Exmouth; 6 between Sidmouth Junction and Exmouth, and 3 down and 2 up between Tipton St John's and Sidmouth, freight workings being similar to other days as were the through workings to Exeter.

On Sundays 11 down and 12 up trains ran, and also one each way between Sidmouth and Exmouth. One working was through to Sidmouth from Axminster. The branch journey time for passenger trains varied from 20 to 23 minutes.

The loads of trains worked by one engine between Tipton St John's and Sidmouth stations were:

A female booking clerk, 1941, dates a ticket with an Edmonson machine. Racks of tickets are on each side of the window. The last letters of 'Sidmouth Junction' can be seen in reverse to her left. *Author's Collection*

Class '2MT' 2-6-2T No. 41318, shedded at Exmouth Junction, leaves for Sidmouth with the 10.55 am departure on 31st May, 1963, watched by the signalman. *J.H. Aston*

'M7' class 0-4-4T No. 30025 (of Exmouth Junction) and BR Standard class '3MT' 2-6-2T No. 82019, leave Sidmouth Jn for Sidmouth and Exmouth with the 11.45 am Saturdays-only ex Waterloo on 1st August, 1953.   *J.H. Bamsey*

View south from the footbridge at Tipton St John's on 30th May, 1936, prior to the junction being modified. The Sidmouth train climbs the gradient of 1 in 45 as the level crossing gates are opened to road traffic.   *S.W. Baker*

A Vauxhall Victor waits at the level crossing at Tipton St John's for the 4.5 pm Exmouth to Sidmouth to arrive at the down platform, 25th February, 1967. The train will reverse and continue to Sidmouth. Note the modified junction. *R.A. Lumber*

'M7' class 0-4-4T No. 30670 stands at Sidmouth in August 1953. The corridor coach next to the engine is in carmine and cream livery. Three rows of fire buckets stand behind the stop blocks. *John Edgington*

Down Trains - Tipton St John's-Sidmouth:

Passenger	'02' class	128 tons
Passenger	'T1' class	150 tons
Passenger	'M7' class	160 tons

Goods: Not exceeding equal to 16 loaded goods wagons and 1 heavy brake van or 2 light vans.

Mixed: 64 tons equal to 6 loaded goods wagons and 1 heavy brake.

Up Trains - Sidmouth-Tipton St John's:

Passenger	'02' class	150 tons
Passenger	'T1' class	170 tons
Passenger	'M7' class	180 tons

Goods: Not exceeding equal to 28 loaded wagons and 1 heavy brake van or 2 light vans with a guard in each.

Mixed: 64 tons equal to 6 loaded goods wagons and 1 brake van.

Goods trains between Tipton St John's and Sidmouth had to have a heavy brake van of not less than 20 tons at the rear of the train, fitted if possible with sanding gear. If this heavy brake was not available, two smaller brake vans with a guard in each had to be provided.

The winter 1938-9 service consisted of 23 trains each way on weekdays and was virtually identical to the summer Monday-Friday timetable. No Sunday trains were scheduled until 7th May, 1939, when three each way were introduced. In the summer of 1939 trains from Sidmouth Junction to Sidmouth took 22-30 minutes each way and ran as follows:- Down: 14 weekdays, 19 Saturdays, 13 Sundays; Up: 15 weekdays, 14 Saturdays, 13 Sundays.

The basic service remained during the war and by the summer of 1948 had become 13 down and 12 up trains, increasing to 15 and 14 respectively on Saturdays. There was also one working each way between Tipton St John's and Sidmouth. The Sunday service consisted of seven trains each way plus four between Tipton St John's and Sidmouth, the latter being to or from Exmouth. The Sunday service to Sidmouth had increased to nine by 1949.

By 1951, 15 trains each way were being provided on Mondays to Fridays, rising to 20 down and 18 up on Saturdays. Twelve ran each way on Sundays including three through to or from Exmouth. Four return workings were shown for that winter on Sundays, but these were later cut back to start at Easter.

With the introduction of diesel multiple unit trains on 4th November, 1963, only second class accommodation was provided on most trains, though

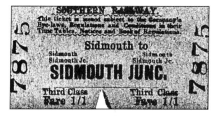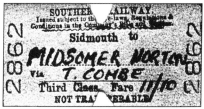

Reproductions of tickets used over the line in Southern Railway days.

Eastern Region coaches stand on the right, awaiting the Saturdays-only service to Cleethorpes. The platform canopy is supported on uprights of old rail. The end of the canopy bears a warning: 'This roof covering is fragile. For your safety use permanent walking ways, duck or roof ladders, knee or crawling boards'.   *Lens of Sutton*

A dmu has just arrived at Sidmouth on 8th June, 1964. Notice the decorative brackets to the canopy supports.   *Author's Collection*

through coaches providing two classes ran on summer Saturdays until 1965. The Summer 1964 timetable showed 11 down and 10 up trains Mondays to Fridays, plus one each way between Sidmouth and Exmouth.

On Saturdays this increased to 19 down and 21 up, including two each way between Sidmouth and Exmouth.

The Sunday service was 10 in each direction. In 1966 the service was reduced to 7 down and 6 up between Sidmouth Junction and Sidmouth, supplemented by three from Exmouth-Sidmouth, four Sidmouth-Exmouth, one Sidmouth Junction-Exmouth and two in the reverse direction, these latter three having Sidmouth connections.

The final summer service showed a slight decrease in through trains, although the seven down and five up on Mondays-Fridays, eleven and nine on Saturdays and six and seven on Sundays were increased by several Exmouth-Sidmouth Junction or Sidmouth return workings, connecting at Tipton St John's in some cases. The Sunday service that year ran from 22nd May to 25th September only.

The summer 1938 timetable showed through coaches on Mondays to Fridays to both Sidmouth and Exmouth on the 11.00 am and 3.00 pm from Waterloo, and to Sidmouth only on the 1.00 pm from Waterloo. On Saturdays there were coaches on the 8.38 am, 9.01 am, 12.00 noon and 3.00 pm trains. There was also the 10.24 am Derby-Sidmouth and Exmouth via Bath and the Somerset & Dorset line, joining the Southern Railway at Templecombe. On Sundays, through coaches ran on the 11.00 am ex-Waterloo.

In the up direction through coaches joined the 10.30 am and 12.45 pm from Exeter Central, while on Saturdays the service was increased so that coaches were added to the 9.55 and 11.05 am from Exeter and there was also a 2.20 pm ex-Sidmouth. The Derby through coaches were attached to the 9.30 am from Exeter. This last service was not resumed after the war. In the winter of 1952-3 Sidmouth was served by a coach from the down 'Atlantic Coast Express' but with no balancing up working. In the summer of 1953 there were three through Saturday trains from Waterloo to Exmouth and Sidmouth, all of which were reversed at Sidmouth Junction and double-headed to Tipton St John's, where they were divided. The 8.05 am from Waterloo consisted of no more than a total of seven bogie coaches, so each part was taken beyond Tipton by one of the two engines. The 9.00 am however with 12 coaches, required its 7-coach Exmouth portion to be taken on by the two engines, while another hauled the remaining five coaches to Sidmouth. The 11.45 am had eight coaches for Exmouth and four for Sidmouth.

In 1960 the destination of the 7.00 am ex-Cleethorpes was transferred from Bournemouth to Sidmouth and Exmouth, and this train, running via Bath and over the Somerset & Dorset line, reached Sidmouth at 5.17 pm. The return working was at 11.07 am from Sidmouth, arriving at Cleethorpes at 9.30 pm. This service finished on 1st September, 1962 when the Somerset & Dorset ceased to be used by long distance trains.

In 1960, at about 10.30 am, six tank engines could be seen in sidings at Sidmouth Junction. Two had come up on the 9.25 am Sidmouth-Waterloo, two on the 9.25 am Exmouth-Waterloo, one on the 9.38 am Littleham-Waterloo and one on the 10.17 am ex-Sidmouth. In the summer of 1963 the 9.32 am from Sidmouth and 9.10 am from Littleham were combined at Sidmouth Junction. The Monday to Friday through coaches were withdrawn in 1964 and the remainder in 1966.

At Sidmouth Junction a flagman positioned at the west end of the down platform waved a train over the level crossing until he judged that the rear coaches to be detached had sufficiently cleared the points at the east end to allow the branch engine to come on the rear and remove the coaches. When he estimated that the rear coaches were at the correct place, he changed his green flag for a red one. At Sidmouth Junction, the two coaches off the 'Atlantic Coast Express' were coupled to two others and worked to Tipton St John's where the Exmouth coach was uncoupled, the remainder proceeding to Sidmouth. A two-coach set then coupled on to the through coach and the three travelled to Exmouth. The through coach from Waterloo to Exmouth was at various times part of three different trains.

Engines of through main line trains destined for Sidmouth or Exmouth, were detached at Sidmouth Junction and run light to Exmouth Junction shed for servicing.

An interesting working in the summer of 1964 was a Sundays-only dmu from Tiverton to Sidmouth via Exmouth, the return working being only from Exmouth.

The 8.35 am from Sidmouth ran primarily for the benefit of pupils of King's School, Ottery St Mary, and for some years terminated at that station. The number of pupils using the train grew to such an extent that a third coach, usually a non-corridor ex-LSWR vehicle, was added, but during the week commencing 6th September, 1948, an ex-LNER Tourist open saloon appeared on the afternoon train. Scholars returned to Sidmouth by the 3.38 pm which was rostered to be hauled by the 'M7' locomotive that had shunted in the yard at Honiton during the day, but the time it actually ran depended on when this work finished. Boys and girls spent anxious moments waiting to see if the 3.20 pm from Sidmouth which was scheduled to cross at Ottery, was allowed to run on to Sidmouth Junction, resulting in the down train being at least 20 minutes late.

With the commencement of the summer timetable of 16th June, 1947, the train to Sidmouth left 27 minutes later and as school leaving time was also made later, this resulted in pupils bound for Honiton missing their normal train. A coach was therefore put on the branch freight and after a brake van had been attached at Sidmouth Junction, was worked on to Honiton by the engine of the 5.18 pm milk train to Waterloo, usually a Salisbury 'N15' of the 448-457 series. By 1951 services had been altered so that on the branch the children could catch the 3.50 (later 3.43) passenger train from Sidmouth, but the special from Sidmouth Junction to Honiton ran until the closure of the branch.

Freight was mainly agricultural goods, cement and building materials and coal, including supplies for Sidmouth gas works which adjoined the station. Following gas works closure, its sidings were taken over by Devon Conversions which made Caravanettes from Volkswagen vans, these being transported by rail between the docks at Ramsgate and Sidmouth. The daily branch freight train left Sidmouth Junction at 7.20 am and departed from Sidmouth at 3.05 pm calling at intermediate stations as required. Gerneral freight traffic ceased on 6th September, 1965, but coal traffic continued until 8th May, 1967.

At first the branch was worked by staff and ticket under absolute block regulations, but by 1904 Tyer's train tablet system had been introduced.

The 1960 Appendix to the Working Timetable stated that passenger trains on the branch could be worked without a guard as long as the number of coaches did not exceed three.

On 4th September, 1954 Bertram Mills' Circus travelled in six trains from Exmouth to Sidmouth, reversing at Tipton St John's. Two were double-headed from Exmouth to Budleigh Salterton and the remainder banked. By special authority they were permitted to be banked in the rear from Tipton St John's to Sidmouth. Apart from one 'N' class 2-6-0, all the locomotives used were tank engines. After unloading, as there was insufficient siding accommodation at Sidmouth, empty stock was widely dispersed to places ranging from Ottery St Mary to Exmouth Junction. On the night of 7th/8th September, loaded specials left Sidmouth for Dorchester. Two were double-headed and the rest had an engine at each end for braking purposes as far as Tipton St John's, where four of the specials were combined into two. At Sidmouth Junction, two others were amalgamated, only four trains travelling forward to Dorchester.

Class '2MT' 2-6-2T No. 41306 on 13th July, 1960 shunting utility vans containing Volkswagen vehicles *en route* from being imported at Ramsgate to J.P. White's motor caravan works on the site of the former gas works at Sidmouth. There the motor vans will be converted to Devonettes.   *R.C. Riley*

'West Country' Pacific No. 21C110 at Sidmouth before its naming ceremony on 27th June, 1946. Curtains conceal the nameplate 'Sidmouth'. *P.K. Tunks*

Ivatt class '2MT' 2-6-2T No. 41322 running light engine south of Newton Poppleford *en route* to Tipton St John's on 24th August, 1963. *Author*

Chapter Four

Locomotives and Coaches
on the Sidmouth Branch

The August 1874 Working Timetable stipulated that no engines were to be used on the branch other than those constructed to work on 'light' railways, and that their speed was to be restricted to 25 mph. The 'Ilfracombe Goods' 0-6-0 engines had proved so successful when ballasting the Sidmouth line in 1874 that the Locomotive Committee ordered another two, one intended for permanent use on the branch. On 11th May, 1876, No. 283, one of the original engines of this class, struck and killed a bullock which strayed on the line near Tipton St John's. The farmer, not so honest as he should have been, sold the carcase to a butcher at Budleigh Salterton for £8 and charged the railway company £28. The LSWR had to invoke the assistance of the law to reclaim this sum and expenses. No. 283 was still allocated to Sidmouth in March 1878.

Standard Beattie 2-4-0 well tanks also worked the branch trains at an early date. By about 1890 Adams '02' class 0-4-4 tank engines had replaced the 'Ilfracombe Goods' on the Sidmouth line. A report to Adams dated September 1893 regarding those members of the class working on West of England branches, showed them as being well-suited for such duties, in addition to burning 16 per cent less fuel than Beattie well tanks and suffering 34 per cent fewer failures. In 1901 'G6' class 0-6-0Ts Nos. 270/4/5/8/9 worked the Sidmouth and Budleigh Salterton goods trains.

In the spring of 1903 before opening of the branch to Lyme Regis, ex-LBSCR 'Terrier' 0-6-0T No. 734 purchased by the LSWR for operating that branch worked on the Sidmouth line and was still noted working there on August Bank Holiday Monday. Following the opening of the Lyme Regis branch, one of the two 'Terriers' (Nos. 734/5) kept as spare, worked, among other duties, goods to Sidmouth. By mid-1909, '02' class 0-4-4Ts had taken over Lyme Regis branch trains and No. 734 was sub-shedded at Sidmouth for a few months; No. 735 worked Sidmouth Junction-Sidmouth-Exmouth trains. Soon both were transferred from the area. Following the introduction of '0415' class 4-4-2Ts on the Lyme Regis branch in 1913, three of these engines were based at Exmouth Junction, one sometimes appearing on the Sidmouth line.

Early in 1932, '02' class 0-4-4Ts Nos. 178/81/91/98, 203/7/8/14/31/35 could be found working Exeter-Exmouth-Sidmouth services, but by the middle of that year Drummond 0-4-4Ts had appeared and ousted many of the '02s', some of which were soon condemned at Eastleigh. In mid-1937 'M7s' class locomotives shedded at Exmouth Junction were Nos. 24, 34/7/9, 44, 123/4, 133, 256, 321/3, 356, 374/5/6/7, 669, 671. Five worked Exeter-Exmouth-Sidmouth; two (1 Saturdays-only) Sidmouth-Honiton-Axminster; two Exeter-Exmouth-Sidmouth Junction and one Sidmouth-Sidmouth Junction. During World War II some '02' class were still to be found on the branch and these were Nos. 193, 224, 230/2. Among the 'M7s' which appeared were Nos. 46, 124, 133, 256, 320, 356 (a particular favourite), 375/6/7 and 669. On at least one occasion during the war an 'M7' class locomotive hauled 37 wagons from Sidmouth Junction to

BR Standard class '4MT' 2-6-4T No. 80067 leaves Tipton St John's on the 3.53 pm Sidmouth Junction to Sidmouth, 21st September, 1963. *R.A. Lumber*

Birmingham Railway Carriage & Wagon Co. Suburban Motor Brake Second No. W51329 heads the 2-car unit working the 5.42 pm Sidmouth to Sidmouth Junction on 9th May, 1964. *Author*

Tipton St John's.

In July 1939 Adams' '0395' class 0-6-0 locomotives Nos. 3029 and 3433 had no weekday duties, but worked the 8.52 am Saturdays-only goods from Exmouth Junction to Whimple, ran light to Sidmouth Junction to work the 1.18 pm passenger to Sidmouth, a through train from Waterloo. The engine returned with the 3.45 pm goods to Sidmouth Junction and Exmouth Junction. Freight trains on the branch tended to be hauled by six-coupled engines. On 9th June, 1947 a weed killing train was hauled by 'M7' class No. 49 and '0415' class No. 3488 - the first of the only two recorded visits of a locomotive of this type around this period. The first sign of railway Nationalisation on the branch was on 7th February, 1948, when an 'M7' appeared numbered S668.

'M7' class locomotives fitted for push-pull working appeared on the branch, and in the British Railways period so did ex-LMS Ivatt class '2MT' 2-6-2 tank engines including Nos. 41307 and 41323, BR Standard '2MT' 2-6-2 tank engine No. 84020, BR Standard '3MT' 2-6-2 tank engines Nos. 82010/3/8 and 82036 among others, and also class '4MT' 2-6-4 tank engines including Nos. 80039 and 80067. The 'M7s' were authorised to haul 180 tons from Sidmouth to Tipton, but only 160 tons in the reverse direction. Class '3MT' 2-6-2Ts could take 200 tons.

'West Country' class 4-6-2 No. 21C110 *Sidmouth* traversed the branch on 27th June, 1946 for its naming ceremony, but normally engines of this type were not permitted to use the line. At the ceremony guests were entertained to a meal in a restaurant car. Mr Lancaster Smith, who performed the naming, was presented with a coffee table bearing the appropriate crest and the locomotive's photograph autographed by the Chairman of the Southern Railway, Colonel Gore Brown; the General Manager, Sir Eustace Missenden and the designer, O.V. Bulleid. At the tea following the ceremony at Sidmouth, a particularly welcome guest was Lieut Col E.C. Cox, a former traffic manager, who resided in the town. By the time 21C145 was named *Ottery St Mary*, enthusiasm for these ceremonies had waned. By 1951 permission had been given for light Pacifics and Moguls to use the line subject to a speed limit of 40 mph but Pacifics were infrequent visitors.

On August Bank Holiday 1959 No. 34104 *Bere Alston* assisted by BR Standard class '3MT' 2-6-2T No. 82017, arrived at Sidmouth with the 9-coach City of Plymouth Holiday Express, while at about the same period No. 34011 *Tavistock* was noted on a branch freight train. 'L11' class 4-4-0 engines Nos. 413, 436 and 'K10' Nos. 137/8 have worked passenger trains on the branch; 2-6-0s were rare although 'N' class No. 1840 appeared hauling a freight on 23rd April, 1948 and 'U' class No. 1807 on 5th July the same year. A WR 0-6-0PT headed a Locomotive Club of Great Britain railtour on Sundays 28th February and 7th March, 1965.

It is interesting to note that SR diesel shunters Nos. 15201-3 were banned from the line, but not their lighter BR counterparts Nos. 15211-36, though none however actually appeared. The branch was 'dieselised' on 4th November, 1963 using multiple units and these were restricted to a maximum speed of 50 mph between Sidmouth Junction and Tipton St John's and 40 mph between Tipton and Sidmouth. Beyer Peacock 'Hymek' and North British Type 2 diesel

On 9th September, 1964, dmus cross at Tipton St John's: Swindon Cross Country Motor Second W51588 *right*, 5.51 pm Tipton St John's to Exmouth; Birmingham Carriage & Wagon Co. Suburban Motor Second W51329, *left*, on the 5.42 pm Sidmouth to Sidmouth Junction. *Author*

A 2-car dmu leaves as the 3.53 pm to Sidmouth Junction on 4th March, 1967, the last day of passenger working. Some points of interest are: the goods shed behind the second coach; the solitary coal wagon in the yard. A building on the left has doors above ground level for easy transfer to and from railway wagons. *R.A. Lumber*

locomotives worked the summer Saturday London trains, though in 1964, at least some of the Saturdays-only services, and the 9.23 am ex-Waterloo Sunday excursion, were still steam-hauled over the branch.

Headcodes used on the branch were a disc on the near-side mid-iron from 1st January, 1892 and the disc on the off-side mid-iron from 1st May, 1901.

The engine shed provided when the branch opened was a small timber structure about 45 ft by 18 ft, the roof being slated. Entrance to the shed was across a 42 ft diameter turntable. Early one Sunday in January 1900 the building went up in flames, the locomotive superintendent Dugald Drummond reporting: ' . . . at 1 o'clock on the morning of 7th instant the engine shed at Sidmouth was destroyed by fire, the origin of which is unknown, and the engine No. 195 which was stabled there was slightly damaged. The cost of the repairs is estimated at £200.' On discovering the fire, Falkner the station master living in the nearby station house, promptly summoned the staff who worked hard to subdue the flames, but it was a hopeless job. Apart from having its paint burnt off, the '02' class locomotive was little damaged and was prepared to work the services that day before being returned that evening to Exmouth Junction where, later in the month, she was repainted. Sidmouth shed was rebuilt in brick but ceased to be used by locomotives in the 1930s, the turntable being removed about this time. The building is still used by an engineering firm.

After the disappearance of 6-wheeled stock around 1920, ex-LSWR 2-coach non-corridor sets were used on the branch comprising a 5-compartment 3rd brake and a 5-compartment corridor brake. These were in general use on local passenger trains in the Exeter area. From about 1936 onwards, the sets consisted of an LSWR brake composite and a 61 ft 7 in. rebuilt LSWR brake third on an SR underframe. In the case of five of the sets (Nos. 42-46), both coaches were 61 ft 7 in. rebuilds. Later the non-corridor coaches were withdrawn, and various combinations were formed into two-coach sets, e.g.: rebuilt LSWR brake third and LSWR corridor brake composite; 59 ft 7in. LSWR brake third and rebuilt LSWR composite; 59 ft 7 in. LSWR brake third and SECR composite; LSWR brake third and Maunsell corridor brake composite. Both Maunsell and Bulleid stock in a variety of combinations worked branch and through Waterloo services, while ex-LNER Gresley and Thompson stock was used on the Cleethorpes service, together with BR Mark I regional variants. Some local services used the latest BR Standard suburban compartment stock.

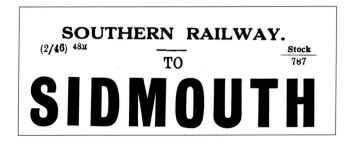

SOUTHERN RAILWAY.

(2/46) 48ᴹ

Stock

TO   787

SIDMOUTH

'02' class 0-4-4T locomotive No. 359 driven by Mrs Williams Drummond, arrives at Budleigh Salterton with the inaugural train, 14th May, 1897.   *Fairlynch Museum*

An '02' class 0-4-4T locomotive at Budleigh Salterton, *c.* 1905. Note the locomotive headcode.
Author's Collection

Chapter Five

History of the
Budleigh Salterton Railway

Shortly after the Sidmouth Railway was planned, in 1862 a scheme was put forward to build, from a junction at Tipton St John's, the Sidmouth, Budleigh Salterton & Exmouth Railway. Ideas were simplified and the Sidmouth & Budleigh Salterton Railway Act of 28th July, 1863, 26 & 27 Vic. cap. 234, authorised the building of a line from Tipton only as far as Budleigh Salterton and the raising of a capital of £80,000 and borrowing powers of £26,600; arrangements were permitted to be made with the LSWR to work the line. The scheme failed to make headway and three years later, a similar plan, though with modifications near Knowle, was put forward with the LSWR's Consulting Engineer, W.R. Galbraith and his partner J.H. Tolmé. A deviation in the Harpford-Colaton Raleigh area was authorised by the Sidmouth & Budleigh Salterton Railway Act, 28 & 29, Vic. cap. 282 of 5th July, 1865; however the scheme was abortive.

The next attempt was an extension from Sidmouth itself and would have been worked by the LSWR, under terms similar to that for the Sidmouth Railway, the agreement being dated 19th May, 1876. The Sidmouth Railway Act of 11th August, 1876, 39 & 40 Vic. cap. 210, permitted the construction of a line from Sidmouth station, making a junction with the newly-opened Sidmouth Railway and requiring the construction of a curving platform west of the existing one, necessitating a slight deviation of the road outside the station. The line was to run parallel with the coast, a 475 yards-long tunnel penetrating Peak Hill and would have then crossed the River Otter near East Budleigh and followed the approximate course of the railway as it was later built, making a junction with the Exeter & Exmouth Railway near its terminus. This expensive line, with its heavy earthworks, failed to materialise when the Sidmouth Company found it impracticable to raise the authorised capital of £130,000 and the Sidmouth Railway Act, Vic. 42 & 43, which received Royal Assent on 23rd May, 1879, allowed the abandonment of the lines authorised in 1876.

The proposal was far from forgotten and a meeting held at the Rolle Hotel, Exmouth on 9th December, 1882 was well attended. Dr T.N. Brushfield presided and Dr Crompton read the report of a committee appointed to take steps to obtain railway communication to Budleigh Salterton. It was a record of hard work, frustration and failure. A request for assistance from the local estate owner, the Hon. Mark Rolle, had met with a courteous and satisfactory reply. A memorial had also been addressed to the LSWR Directors setting forth the claims and advantages of a railway from Salterton to Exmouth starting at the foot of the Burlow Almshouses, this position being selected and agreed as being as convenient as Moor Lane and far less expensive. The deputation was courteously received by the Directors, but it appeared that the LSWR shareholders were so opposed to extensions that the Board could not consider any suggestions except with a great inducement such as an offer of the land, or other similar proposals. The committee had reason to believe that the Hon. Mark Rolle would give the land between the foot of the Common as far as the divergence into the Withycombe valley at the termination of the Rolle property.

Mr R.H. Lipscomb, the Rolle Estate agent, considered the value of the land somewhere between £600 and £700, but the committee pointed out that the Directors could not be tempted by such an offer even if made.

It also pointed out that Lipscomb would not submit to the proposal to enter Exmouth by the Withycombe valley. The committee did not know whether terms more advantageous to the LSWR had been made privately by the Rolle Estate, but it felt the Directors had done all that a body of gentlemen could do, fettered by the known feeling of their shareholders against extensions at the expense of the company. 'All the committee know', the report concluded, 'is that their efforts have been so far fruitless and they beg to resign their office, except it is your pleasure that a further effort should be made.'

Dr Crompton, commenting on the report, said that a railway engineer had offered to come down at no expense to the company and go into the question of a tunnel into Exmouth. He had communicated this offer to Lipscomb, who had neither acknowledged the receipt of the letter, nor it appeared communicated with the engineer. Mr Leslie, a London shareholder in the LSWR, believed Budleigh Salterton might benefit if the Great Western and the LSWR could have been brought into conflict and it was suggested that the Great Western might be induced to build a branch from Cullompton. It was felt that the true feeder of Budleigh Salterton, Exmouth and Sidmouth, was not the LSWR but the GWR, which had the benefit of direct communication with the Midlands and the North.

The next attempt to secure a line was in 1886 when W. Lidstone and H.T. Munday planned a line from Tipton St John's station to a terminus at Budleigh Salterton, midway between the village and Otterton Point. This scheme had the advantage of only requiring a relatively easy section of line along the valley floor of the Otter. On 1st December, 1886 a public meeting was called to discuss the matter, a postscript curiously adding 'Boys and girls not admitted'.

At this same meeting it was pointed out that the Bill had been replaced in Parliament and a deposit of £2,400 8s. 1d. made. 'The promoters,' the ultimatum stated, 'have already spent nearly £3,000, not a farthing of which has been contributed by the district. It will cost a further sum of £500 to carry the Bill through Parliament. The Hon. Mark Rolle has promised to do what he can to forward the scheme. It now rests entirely with you as to whether the line is made or not.' One outcome of this meeting was that leaflets were printed appealing to residents to take as many £10 shares as they could afford, warning that 'unless a moderate amount of capital be promised from Devonshire, it will be impossible to raise the further sum to complete the £50,000 which the line will cost.'

Although Lidstone and Munday's project also failed to get Parliamentary approval, it led the way for a similar scheme in 1893 which had William Clarke as Engineer. Exmouth Dock Company was its chief opponent and said that the amount of Dock income received by goods carried from Exmouth to Budleigh was about £500 yearly and that if they were to lose this, their net income would fall to £1,500 per annum and be only sufficient to cover the debenture interest. George Ellett, Managing Director of the Dock Company and a tenant of the Rolle Estate, said that he was one of the largest shareholders in the company and would not have made his investment had he anticipated a railway being built. This was a conflict of tenant and landlord, as the Hon. Mark Rolle was a Director of the railway company. Exmouth Local Board, of which Ellett was Chairman, passed a resolution:

> That this Board expresses its opinion that the construction of a line of railway from Tipton to Budleigh Salterton (notices of an application for an Act of Parliament for which had been advertised) will be very detrimental to the trade and interests of the town of Exmouth and will considerably damage and lessen the value of the property there and will be very prejudicial to its increasing growth and prosperity. The Board therefore consider it their duty as representing the town, to take all steps within its power to oppose the passing of the Act.

However, the determination of the Salterton people outweighed Exmouth's opposition. For instance, Harry Perriam, grocer and merchant of High Street, Budleigh Salterton, wrote a letter supporting the town's claim to have a railway. In it he said that his trade was principally with London, Bristol and Exeter for groceries, and with Burton-on-Trent, Shepton Mallet and Weymouth for beer. 'I have looked out my carriage bills for 1893 and I find that my tonnage for beer alone was 73 tons 3 cwt and my total tonnage about 130. All this had to be hauled from Exmouth station. The South Western Railway Company's agent's minimum charge for carriage is 4*d.* per hundredweight for hauling from Exmouth for heavy goods'. He added that he very rarely had anything delivered at Exmouth Docks. Perriam formed a local committee in Budleigh to support the Bill. The Dock Company made no impression on the Select Committee of the House of Lords and its Chairman gave permission for the Bill to proceed without retiring.

On 20th July, 1894 an Act for the incorporation of the Budleigh Salterton Railway was passed, 57 & 58 Vic. cap. 100, authorising a line from Tipton to Budleigh. The capital was to be £60,000, with borrowing powers of £20,000, though in the event, only £3,000 of the debenture stock was taken up. The railway could have been built as a light railway, though in actual fact it was not. The first Directors were the Hon. Mark Rolle, Dr Robert Walker, and Dr Thomas Brushfield, (it was most unusual for two-thirds of a railway directorate to be doctors). The Trustees of the Estate, empowered by the Act, guaranteed to augment net receipts for up to 20 years after the line's opening to ensure a dividend of three per cent per annum was paid on called-up capital, these payments being charged at four per cent per annum.

The LSWR undertook to work the line in perpetuity, taking £65 for junction costs and 60 per cent of the balance of gross receipts yearly, paying the rest to the Budleigh company, plus £150 for office expenses.

The first ordinary meeting of the company was held at the Rolle Hotel, East Budleigh, on 19th January,1895. On 6th November, the first sod was cut at Greenway Lane, Budleigh Salterton, by Lady Gertrude Rolle, wife of the landowner through whose property the line passed. Harry Perriam's daughter,

A fine view of Budleigh Salterton, looking towards Exmouth, *c.* 1903. Notice the low signal box and goods shed beyond.   *Exmouth Library*

'02' class 0-4-4T locomotive No. 203 stands at Budleigh Salterton on a down train, *c.* 1930. The engine carries the Exeter to Exmouth headcode. Notice the ¾ mile post against the platform facing.   *Lens of Sutton*

Dora, presented her with a bouquet.

The spade had a solid silver blade and carved ebony handle and was kept in the strongroom of Budleigh Salterton Urban Council. Four hundred navvies employed by Lucas & Aird, set to work. In 1896 the Otter overflowed and washed away temporary bridges erected by the contractor and caused a delay. In September it was decided to call the two stations 'Budleigh' and 'Salterton' and the following year it was agreed to build a station at Newton Poppleford and a siding at Colaton Raleigh. On 13th April, 1897 the venue for the general meetings was changed from the Rolle Hotel, to the Rolle Estate Office, Exmouth.

The contractors, Lucas & Aird, proved an excellent choice as they finished work six months before time. Major F. Marindin inspected the line on behalf of the Board of Trade on 16th April, 1897 travelling in a train of 'two heavy coaches' drawn by 'two large London & South Western engines'. He was thoroughly satisfied with the work and wrote the following report.

RAILWAY DEPARTMENT,
Board of Trade,
April 10th 1897

The Assistant Secretary,
Railway Department,
Board of Trade.

I have the honour to report for the information of the Board of Trade, that in compliance with instructions contained in your Minute of the 2nd Inst, I have inspected the Budleigh Salterton Ry, a single line 6 m. 43.80 ch. in length, from Tipton St John's station on the Sidmouth branch of the L.S.W.Ry to Budleigh Salterton.

Land has been purchased and the overbridges have been constructed for a double line.

The gauge is 4 ft 8½ in. and the width of formation level is 18 feet.

The line is generally fairly level and straight, but there are two 16 chain curves, and one length of 54 chains, near the terminus at Budleigh Salterton, upon a gradient of 1 in 50.

There is one embankment with a height of 44 ft and one cutting with a depth of 36 ft, but as a rule the cuttings and embankments and the works generally are light.

The rails are double-headed steel rails weighing 82 lb. per yard, and the chairs, each of which has three fastenings, weigh 40 lb. each.

The sleepers are creosoted Memel timber and they are laid 2 ft 2 in. apart at the joints and from 2 ft 5 in. to 2 ft 10 in. apart elsewhere.

The ballast is of good quality and is ample in quantity.

Post and rail fencing has been used.

There are stations at Budleigh and at Salterton, both of which have single platforms only, and there are siding connections at Newton Poppleford - 1 m. 13 ch., and Collaton Raleigh [sic] 3 m. 3 ch.

There are no signals except at Salterton, all the points connected with the main line being worked from ground frames locked by the Train Staff.

The accommodation provided at stations is sufficient.

There is no engine turntable at either end of the new line.

There are 16 underbridges - all of which have cast-iron superstructure, the others having brich arches, the widest of which has a span of 22 ft 7½ in. The only bridges of any importance are three across the River Otter with spans of 54 ft 8 in.; 65 ft and 80 ft respectively.

Between 4 m. 5 ch. and 5 m. 12 ch. the line has been laid outside the limits of the deviation, but this has been done by consent of the landowner thro' whose land the line runs for nearly its whole length. The line has been decidedly improved by the alteration and I see no reason to object to it, but it is a question whether a certificate should not be applied for.

There are 6 overbridges all but one with brick faced concrete abutments. Three have cast-iron superstructures, widest span 30 ft; two have each 3 arches of 26 feet span; and the remaining one, a footbridge, is constructed entirely of timber.

All these works are well and substantially constructed and were satisfactorily tested. The line is well finished throughout, and, subject to the provision of;

1. An undertaking to work the line with One Engine in Steam carrying a Staff.
2. An undertaking to stop all trains at the intermediate station, there being no turntables.

I can recommend that it may be opened for passenger traffic. The speed at first should not be high, for although there is a remarkably firm top upon the line, it has not yet been run over by heavy engines, and it is desirable that if possible it should be worked by Tank Engines.

I have the honour to be Sir,
Yr. Obt. Servant,
F. Marindin Maj. R.E.

On 14th May a special train of five coaches brought LSWR officials from Waterloo for the ceremonial opening and reached Sidmouth Junction at 12.12 pm. Here it was coupled to a special train from Exeter which had left that city at 11.45 am with a saloon and van. Mrs Hugh Williams Drummond, daughter of the Hon. Mark Rolle, and wife of the company's Chairman, 'drove' this inaugural train, headed by No. 359, a 'T1' class 0-4-4 tank engine decorated with flags, evergreens and the portrait of Mrs Williams Drummond. At Tipton, the village schoolmaster conducted his pupils singing the National Anthem, and as it left the station and started on the branch proper, it exploded fog signals. Unfortunately Mrs Williams Drummond overran (East) Budleigh station and had to set back. The train was welcomed at (Budleigh) Salterton both by the strains of the Sidmouth Volunteers' Band and by civic officials. Mrs Williams Drummond declared the line open and her husband formally handed it over to Wyndham S. Portal, the LSWR Chairman. Then followed the luncheon. The day was a public holiday and many of the streets and houses were decorated, a free tea being provided for children under fourteen. The (East) Budleigh station master was Mr Larcombe, late inspector from Ilfracombe, his counterpart at (Budleigh) Salterton being Mr T. Russell, formerly booking clerk at Ilfracombe.

It was the Budleigh Salterton Railway which brought Brigadier-General Sir Hugh Drummond, Bart, MVO, partner in the Exeter Bank, into contact with the LSWR and which led to him becoming an LSWR Director in 1900, Deputy Chairman in 1904 and Chairman in 1911.

In November 1898 the LSWR had declined Drummond's offer to dispose of the controlling interest in the Budleigh Salterton Railway, but in 1910, when the LSWR had experienced how traffic had developed, it offered to purchase the line. The agreement was confirmed by the LSWR Act of 18th August, 1911, the transfer being effective on 1st January, 1912, when the Budleigh Salterton Railway's share capital of £60,000 was exchanged for LSWR three per cent debentures.

The line saw a good volume of traffic. In 1951 8,133 tickets were issued, rising to approximately 28,000 in 1962, but following this success, British Railways changed train timings with the result that figures dropped by half. In 1965 about 145 tickets were issued daily in summer and a mere 16 in winter. The first public notices of withdrawal were published in August 1964, the Ministry of Transport announcing the following year that closure would not take place until additional bus services had been authorised. The Devon General Omnibus & Touring Company Ltd agreed in February 1967 to operate extra buses and final closure notices were issued that month, train services being withdrawn on 6th March, 1967.

A view of East Budleigh station, looking towards Exmouth on 4th September, 1958. To the left of the nameboard 'for Ladram Bay' appears on the garden in pebbles. Beyond the passenger station is a cattle feed store, the food arriving by rail and distributed by road. Notice the railwaymen's allotments to the left of the line.   *H.B. Priestley*

BUDLEIGH SALTERTON BRANCH

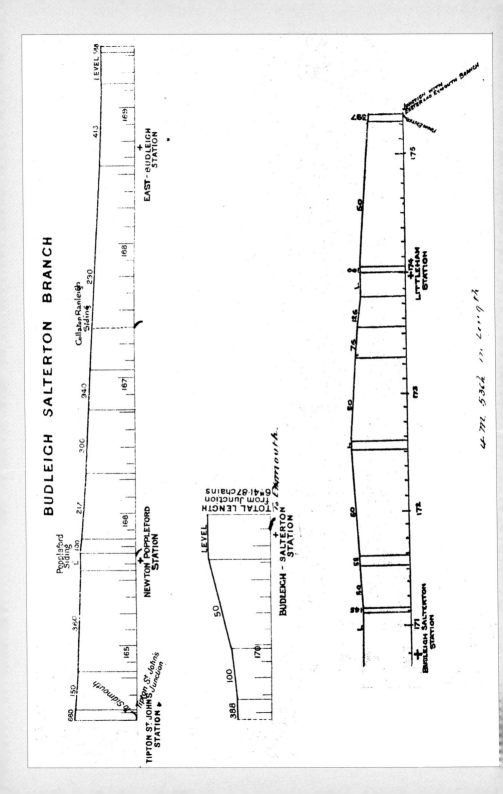

6 m. 53 ch. in Length

Chapter Six

The Extension from Budleigh Salterton to Exmouth

In November 1896 the Rolle Trustees proposed that the line be extended to Exmouth and a formal agreement was signed on 24th June, 1898. This was after the opposition of the Budleigh Salterton Railway and that of Exmouth had been overcome, for the original plan was that the line should run from Exmouth station via Imperial Road and the Manor House Grounds, to a tunnel under the Beacon and so on through the Littleham Valley and the cliffs to Budleigh Salterton. The people of Exmouth would not countenance having their town divided in half by a railway and said so in no uncertain terms in a petition to the Hon. Mark Rolle. Their determination prevailed and engineers were forced to adopt the far more expensive alternative route with its tremendous cuttings and viaducts and pass through Marpool Park to Littleham Cross. Half of Sir John Phear's Marpool Estate was subsequently given to the town by the railway, the other half being bought by the council.

The LSWR Act 61 & 62 Vic. cap. 103 of 25th July, 1898 gave authority for the construction of the 4 mile 46.3 chain Exmouth & Salterton Railway. It granted the Hon. Mark Rolle sanction under his agreement dated 24th June, 1898 to convey land for the line without any payment or consideration. When work began in 1899, the *South Western Gazette* commented: 'No Royal Presence, no Duke or Duchess with silver spade, no Director, not even an officer of the company, but only an office boy out of bounds witnessed the cutting of the first sod on one of the prettiest five miles of railway in the sunny south'. The contractor was Henry Lovatt & Sons who had also built sections of the Manchester Ship Canal and the Great Central Railway. The line was constructed under the direction of J.W. Jacomb-Hood, assisted by E. Roach, Resident Engineer. The line was very expensive to construct, costly works being the 30 ft high brick viaduct at Exmouth from Mudbank to Marpool Park, a distance of nearly ¼ mile, the Park being purchased by the LSWR. Another expensive work was Knowle cutting and soil excavated from here was dumped on the foreshore near Exmouth station. It quickly built up to road level and so provided a site on which the new Exmouth goods depot was later built. Hundreds of navvies were needed for the line's construction and a mission was set up in the King's Cinema, Exeter Road, Exmouth, which, aptly, had just been converted from the abandoned St Margaret's Church. Later, it became the Grand, then Royal Cinema before demolition in the early 1980s.

Navvies were looked after by an affable, friendly and somewhat bucolic old-fashioned constable named George Weeks who never brought a man before the magistrates, never experienced any bother with them and was by no means averse to taking a drink in their company. Although his methods were unorthodox, they certainly worked. By June 1901 the deep cutting in Marpool Park had been started and at the Salterton end, the work of making the heavy embankment on the south side of Dalditch Lane was in full swing, and the steam navvy at the same spot was making its way towards Knowle Hill. The

Dalditch Bridge, west of Budleigh Salterton station, *c.* 1903. *Exmouth Library*

Track laying at the line's summit, Knowle Bridge, *c.* 1902. There appears to be a water tank on the left for the contractor's engines. *Author's Collection*

deviation road in Greenway Lane near Salterton station was in a forward state. Another steam navvy had just started cutting through the Exmouth side of Knowle Hill and a locomotive - probably No. 5, an 0-6-0ST built by Hunslet Engine Co. in 1876, works No. 152 - had been conveyed to this section. Spacious accommodation for the men was in the course of erection and water tanks and an engine shed provided. During construction there was a strike for higher wages.

On 21st February, 1902 Godfrey Knight, LSWR Secretary, wrote to the Board of Trade asking if his company might be allowed to use good second-hand 82 lb./yd rails, with an actual weight of not less than 75 lb./yd, as the company anticipated traffic would be 'of a very light description'. His argument continued: 'This was recently allowed by the Board of Trade in the case of the Basingstoke & Alton Light Railway and I shall be glad to hear that the Board will give similar permission in the case of the Exmouth & Salterton Railway'. Major J.W. Pringle replied saying that provided the rails had not, and would not, be turned and that the actual weight of the rails was not less than 75 lb./yd, permission to use second-hand 82 lb. rails was granted. He warned that the Board might find it necessary to impose a speed restriction.

In 1902 plans were rejected for making a triangular junction outside Exmouth in order to allow through running from Exeter to Budleigh Salterton, the price of land being to high. Even so, the total cost of the 4½ miles-long single line was £111,378. The Board of Trade inspector made the following report:

RAILWAY DEPARTMENT,
Board of Trade,
26th May, 1903

The Assistant Secretary,
Railway Department,
Board of Trade.

I have the honour to report for the information of the Board of Trade, that in compliance with the instructions contained in your Minute of the 16th inst, I made an inspection on the 22nd inst, of the new works on the Exmouth and Salterton Railway constructed by the London & S.W. Railway Company under their Act of 1898.

This new line commences at the north end of Exmouth Station and terminates by an end-on junction with the old terminal station of the Company's Tipton St John's and Salterton branch line.

The total length of the new line is 4 miles 44 chains, and the gauge 4 ft 8½ in. There appear to be no deviations outside the limits shown on the deposited plans. The formation has been constructed for a double line of way, width 30 feet, but a single line of rail only has been laid at present, with a crossing loop at Littleham Station.

The steepest gradient has an inclination of 1 in 50, 75 per cent of the line having gradients with this inclination. The line has also considerable curvature (64 per cent) the sharpest curve (at the junction) having a radius of 12 chains, whilst elsewhere curves with a radius of 20 chains occur.

Fencing - This consists in part of posts and rails 4 feet high, and partly of wire, 8 strands, 4½ feet high. It is I consider adequate.

Drainage - The usual side drains and dry rubble drains down the slopes of earth cuttings have been provided.

Earthwork - The new line is carried for the first half through marl clay, and

Knowle Bridge at the line's summit immediately after completion, 1903. Notice the formation, wide enough for a double line. *Exmouth Library*

An excellent picture of the footbridge at Knowle Cutting, view looking east, immediately after completion, 1903. *Exmouth Library*

afterwards through gravel and soil. There are two heavy cuttings each nearly three-quarters of a mile in length, with a maximum depth of 33 feet and 56 feet respectively. The highest embankments occur at 3 miles 50 chains, where the maximum height is 52 feet.

Permanent Way - Second-hand single-headed rails have been used, which when new weighed 82 lb. per yard. The minimum weight of these rails now, I was informed is 79 lb. per yard. The rails rest on cast iron chairs weighing 40 lb. apiece with a bearing area on the sleepers of 87.5 sq. inches. The chairs are secured to the sleepers by three wrought iron (⅞ in.) spikes and oak trenails. The sleepers are of the usual dimensions (9 ft x 10 in x 5 in.) and are creosoted Baltic Fir, 9 sleepers being used to each rail length of 24 feet.

Gravel ballast is used to a stated depth of 12 in. below the sleepers, and the top ballast is of the same material and is adequate in quantity.

Bridging - There are 7 overbridges in all - four of which have three spans each from 26 to 30 feet in length on the square, and the remainder have a single skew span of from 27½ to 43 feet.

There are 7 underbridges each consisting of a single span. Three have segmental arched spans varying in length from 10 to 30 feet, whilst the remainder carry the railway on wrought iron plategirders with pressed floor plates, the largest of these has a skew span of 42 feet.

Viaduct - There is one viaduct (Exmouth viaduct) with a total length of 352 yards. It consists of 23 segmental arches with square spans of 30 feet, and two spans of wrought iron girders with pressed floor plates measuring 43½ and 56½ feet respectively on the skew. The archwork, piers and abutments are built in brick in cement and brick in lime respectively, and the whole has a substantial appearance and shows no sign of weakness. The maximum height is 37½ feet. Recesses are provided in the parapet wall. I tested the wrought iron girder and pressed plate spans under engine load, but as all the bridgework has been constructed for a double line of way, it was impossible to fully test any but the outside girders on one side, with only one pair of lines laid. Such of the girders, however, as were fully loaded gave moderate deflections under test load, and the ironwork has sufficient theoretical strength. When the line is doubled it will be necessary to make further tests at all these iron bridges.

There are 6 culverts of from 3 to 4 feet in diameter.

Level crossings - The only level crossings are two of foot or bridle paths, and one of a private road adjoining Littleham Station which is worked by a gatewheel from the signal cabin and interlocked with the signals.

Stations, signalling and connections.

1. Exmouth Station - The only new work in connection with passenger accommodation has been the lengthening of the island bay platform. The new line forms an additional set of facing points, and all the arrangements of the connections and signalling shown on the diagram are practically new. The signal cabin has been extended, and so also has the lever frame which has been relocked. The frame contains 30 levers of which two are spare.

I have the following requirements to make at this place:-

a. No. 26 lever to be led by either No. 25 or No. 27.
b. No. 30 lever to be led by either No. 28 or No. 29.
c. No. 6 down branch advance starting signal to be removed.
d. The issue of a train tablet at either Littleham or Lympstone to lock Nos. 17 and 19 in their normal position.
e. Shunting on the new branch line to be prohibited.
2. Littleham Station - two platforms have been provided at this new station, and a loop for passing trains. On the up line accommodation for passengers in the

Two views of Littleham station immediately after completion, 1903. (*both*) *Exmouth Library*

shape of a general waiting and booking hall and a ladies' waiting room with conveniences for both sexes have been provided.

The signal cabin is a tablet post, contains a frame with 20 levers of which 2 are spare, and a gatewheel for operating the adjoining level crossing. One of the levers controls a ground frame at the east end of the station, containing two levers from which the east end loop points are worked.

The interlocking is correct.

I have the following requirements to make:-

a.   Self-acting trap points to be provided on the up loop line at the west end at the fouling point with the down line.

b.   Shunting outside the loop line to be prohibited.

c.   Red discs to be fixed to the level crossing gates.

3.   Salterton Station - the new line as stated terminates by an end-on junction with the old line and a passing loop for trains has been provided together with a second (up line) platform on which a waiting shed has been provided. The Company informed me that they have ordered the erection of a footbridge at this station to connect the platforms. The down platform has a general booking hall together with a ladies' waiting room and conveniences for both sexes.

I have the following requirements to make:-

a.   No. 10 to be free of No. 16.

b.   The catch points on the up loop line, and the present up starting signal on the down platform to be removed prior to opening to passenger traffic.

At all these stations the connections require to be properly made to points and signals, and indicating boards and lamps require to be fixed.

The new line is properly equipped for single line working on the electric train tablet system, and an undertaking to work by this method will be required from the Company.

The Company are anxious to open the new line for passenger traffic on 30th June [sic], and have promised to carry out all the above mentioned requirements prior to that date.

On this understanding, and provided that the undertaking referred to is shortly furnished by the Company I can recommend the Board of Trade to approve of the new works.

I have etc.,

J.W. Pringle

The line, together with the intermediate station at Littleham required by the Rolle Trustees, was opened on Whit Monday, lst June, 1903. The first train, four coaches in length, left Exmouth at 6.58 am and so great was the demand that a supplementary one had to be run. The train with dignitaries left at 10.40 and returned from Salterton at noon.   Then followed the customary luncheon (tickets 3s. 6d.), at the Public Hall, Exmouth, (now the Savoy Cinema), with sports in the afternoon. At Salterton there was luncheon at Parker's Cafe and every train on the line was well-filled with passengers. The Rolle Hotel horse bus, hitherto the only passenger conveyance between Exmouth and Salterton, was now superfluous. (In winter it cost 9d. to travel in comparative warmth inside and 6d. to brave the elements on top of the bus, while in summer one suffocated inside for 6d. or enjoyed the fresh air on top for 9d.)

With the development of road transport after World War II the branch became uneconomic. In 1957 the SR envisaged a 20 minute frequency service of diesel-electric multiple-units between Exeter Central and Budleigh Salterton, but the scheme was withdrawn due to the Government setting economy restrictions. The line came under Western Region auspices from 1st January 1963 and the publication that year of the Beeching Report brought the threat of closure nearer.

At Littleham 60 people in winter and 40 in summer used the 7.58 am to Exmouth, the main commuters' train, and the daily average of prams carried between Littleham and Exmouth was 12 to 15. In 1963 1,616 passengers used Budleigh Salterton station each week - an average use by every man, woman and child of once every 16 days. Budleigh Salterton had issued 8,133 tickets in 1951. Eleven years later it issued 27,100 and collected 32,000 tickets, while at Littleham the same year, 15,000 tickets were issued and 17,800 collected. Then changed train timings led to these figures dropping by half. In August 1959 4,195 tickets were collected at Budleigh Salterton, but by the same month in 1965 numbers had fallen to 1,600. That year the station issued about 16 tickets a day during winter and 145 in summer, but 56 passengers used the three trains before 9.00 am, plus another 53 that boarded at Littleham.

From 4th November, 1963 the majority of trains on the branch were diesel units which reduced the operating costs. The annual costs of the line from Tipton St John's to Exmouth were said to be: terminal costs £10,000, movement costs £19,000. Revenue only brought in £8,000 so there was an annual loss of £21,000. Accordingly in August 1964 closure notices were published with details of road services proposed. Closure on 30th November, 1964 was deferred pending the hearing of 83 objections by the Transport Users' Consultative Committee in the Public Hall, Budleigh Salterton on 25th February, 1965.

On 22nd December, 1965 the Minister of Transport gave his consent to closure subject to the completion, by 1st October, 1966, of certain road improvements permitting additional bus services to be introduced as an alternative means of transport. This recognised the view of the Consultative Committee that 'any hardship which would arise from the closures would be substantially removed by the provision of certain proposed additional bus services'. The Ministry also noted that it was 'the Railway Board's intention, so far as may be practicable, to ensure that good bus and rail connections at Honiton are maintained', and that combined bus-rail tickets will be available at Waterloo and Budleigh Salterton.

Assurances were given that rail services would not be withdrawn until road improvements had been carried out, but restrictions on County Council expenditure delayed the completion of these improvements until January 1967. On the twentieth of that month an application for the new replacement bus services was heard by the Traffic Commissioners and granted. Notices of closure dated 31st January were published and the branch closed from 6th March, 1967, but as there was no Sunday service, last trains ran on 4th March. The closing of Tipton St John's meant the end of the West Country's last junction between two single line branches. The replacement bus services were withdrawn a few years later.

On 3rd May, 1967 the District Civil Engineer's Inspection coach ran from Taunton to Exmouth, Sidmouth and Sidmouth Junction, the branch signal boxes having to be opened specially. During August, an Engineer's Department train removed concrete platelayers' huts from the branch, signalling equipment being taken from the boxes on 29th August. Recovery of the Sidmouth and Budleigh branches commenced on 28th May 1968 and from this date a 4.15 am Exeter Central (Platform 4) was run daily, returning at 10.20 Exmouth (Platform 4) to Exeter Riverside, or later in the day if required. The train consisted of a Type 2 North British diesel-hydraulic locomotive of the D63XX series hauling a train of 16 open wagons, two bogie bolster type C wagons and two brake vans. The two bogie bolsters were required to lead from Exmouth. Two former Exmouth signalmen were responsible for the delivery and collection of the token to and from Topsham and accompanied the train on the Salterton line. For the duration of the work, a new two-lever ground frame, released by Annett's key on the wooden train staff, was provided at Exmouth to work the existing facing connection from the branch to No. 4 platform road and the run-round connections were hand operated as the signal box was now out of use. Passenger trains were diverted into No. 2 platform line. The ground frame was installed on 26th May.

The token off the 4.15 am train was returned by road to Topsham by 6.00 am thus locking the train into the Budleigh branch, and collected at 10 am, 2.45 or 9.2 pm for the return train. The two signalmen at Exmouth were also required to indicate where the relief trainmen who left St David's daily at 10.10 by taxi would find their train. It was necessary for the 4.15 am train to be on time otherwise the token would not have been returned in time for the first passenger service. If for any reason the train had not left Exeter Central by 4.45 am, it was required to be cancelled.

The contractors, Stanley Davies Ltd, Edgware, started recovery from the Sidmouth Junction end where connection with the main line had been severed with singling on 11th June, 1967. Work progressed towards Tipton using a Rushton-Bucyrus 22RB crane and a Rolls-Royce powered shunt truck. Wooden and concrete sleepers were loaded into condemned wagons and sent to Yeovil Junction, while traffic open wagons were used for conveying steel sleepers to Briton Ferry and short rail-lengths to Ebbw Vale, Llanwern and Queenborough, bogie bolster type C and 'Borails' carrying rails to Sheffield, Doncaster and Sharpness.

When track lifting had reached Ottery St Mary, severe flooding of the Otter on 10th July breached the Budleigh line at Newton Poppleford and East Budleigh. (Track at the former station had previously been flooded in December 1956.) Rather than repair the breaches, lifting recommenced at East Budleigh on 22nd July and work progressed towards Exmouth leaving two isolated stretches of track (East Budleigh to Ottery St Mary and Tipton St John's to Sidmouth) and some 30 wagons marooned at Tipton. These, together with the permanent way materials, were later removed by road. Track lifting reached Littleham by mid-August and by mid-September was complete. The ground frame at Exmouth was recovered on 20th December and the regular passenger service from Exeter reverted to using platform No. 4.

In 1970, four and a half acres of land, including the former station master's house at Littleham, were bought by the local council to build old people's bungalows, (the new road being called Jarvis Close), and a car park. The cutting at Littleham Cross was partly filled in to allow for an improved road junction, while at Exmouth, part of the viaduct was demolished to carry out the Marpool Hill road improvement scheme, with the remainder being demolished during 1985. A portion of the former trackbed between Littleham and Exmouth was converted first into an amenity walk and then a cycle way.

Littleham station looking towards Tipton St John's, seen from the level crossing, 7th January, 1967.   *E. Wilmshurst*

Chapter Seven

Description of the Line
Tipton St John's to Exmouth

Leaving the junction at Tipton St John's, (164 m. 28 ch.) the line fell on a gradient of 1 in 150, easing to 1 in 360 before crossing the River Otter and proceeding along its right bank to Newton Poppleford, (164 m. 40 ch.). Opened on 1st June, 1899, the station was built of brick, with part of its roof forming the platform awning. The platform, 184 feet in length, was situated on the down side of the single line, at the foot of the hill near the east end of the village, but quite well placed to serve Harpford just across the Otter. The solitary goods siding, worked from a ground frame, had a timber-built cattle cake store. Two camping coaches were placed at the station. In addition to general goods, there was outwards fruit, fruit trees and flower traffic. The station, which closed to freight from 27th January, 1964, was originally staffed by a station master and porter, later just a station master, later still replaced by a leading porter under Ottery St Mary. When the Ottery station master was made redundant, Newton Poppleford was placed under Budleigh Salterton. It was unstaffed from 16th August, 1965.

Beyond the level stretch at Newton Poppleford, the line fell for 10 chains at 1 in 100, easing to 1 in 217/300 and crossing the Otter before flattening to 1 in 940 and then steepening to 1 in 290 before re-crossing the Otter and arriving at Colaton Raleigh Sidings (167 m. 23 ch.). Access to the siding, situated on the up side and serving the village of that name, was governed by a ground frame unlocked by a key on the single line tablet. It was served by up goods trains only and instructions required that a man from East Budleigh assisted with its working. This siding was taken out of use on 1st February, 1953. Up to five wagons of inwards traffic were placed in the siding on behalf of Miller & Lilley who then provided road delivery to local farms, thus avoiding a longer journey from Ottery St Mary.

The gradient continued to descend at 1 in 290, easing to 1 in 413 before East Budleigh, (168 m. 41 ch.), an overbridge immediately east of the station bearing a cast-iron plate 'Joseph Westwood & Co, Engineers, London, 1896'. Despite its name the station was actually nearer the village of Otterton. It is said that it was named East Budleigh and not Otterton so as not to be confused with Otterham, an LSWR station in Cornwall. When opened, the station was simply 'Budleigh', but was re-named on 27th April, 1898. The brick-built station building, still in existence as a private house, stands on the up side of the single line. It has a large awning over the platform and a small brick goods shed on the platform which had a length of 297 feet. To the west was a goods siding with two short spurs, access being from facing and trailing points operated from a ground frame released by electric token. The siding served a concrete cattle cake store belonging to Messrs Silcocks and until the mid-1950s the station despatched hay in open wagons, sheeted and roped. When the number of wagons exceeded the freight's capacity to take them, cattle specials were run from East Budleigh and Ottery St Mary to Maiden Lane, (the slaughterhouse for Smithfield Market).

Newton Poppleford, looking in the down direction, *c.* 1964. Notice the tiles hung on the end of the building. *Lens of Sutton*

Ivatt 2-6-2T No. 41321 arrives at Newton Poppleford with the 11.8 am Tipton St John's to Exmouth train, 10th August, 1963. *Peter W. Grey*

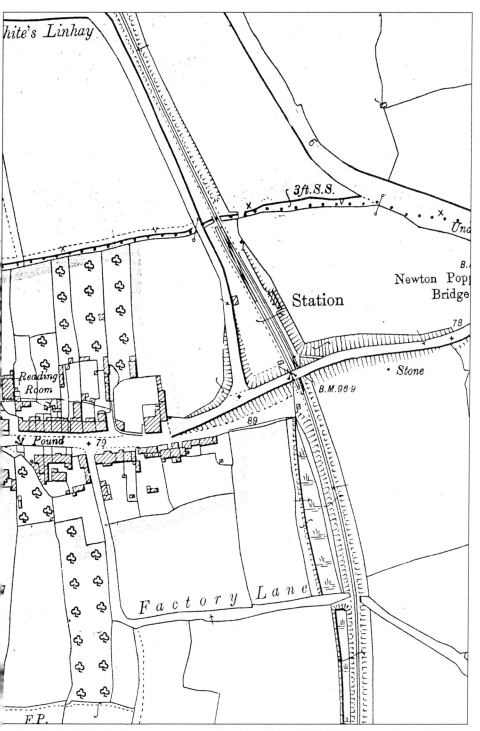

Newton Poppleford station.　　　　*Reproduced from the 25", 1905 Ordnance Survey Map*

Camping coaches at Newton Poppleford: No. 3, *right*; No. 11 *left*; 26th June, 1949.   *J.H. Aston*

Camping coaches at East Budleigh: Nos. 6, *left*, and 11 *right*, 29th June, 1948.   *J.H. Aston*

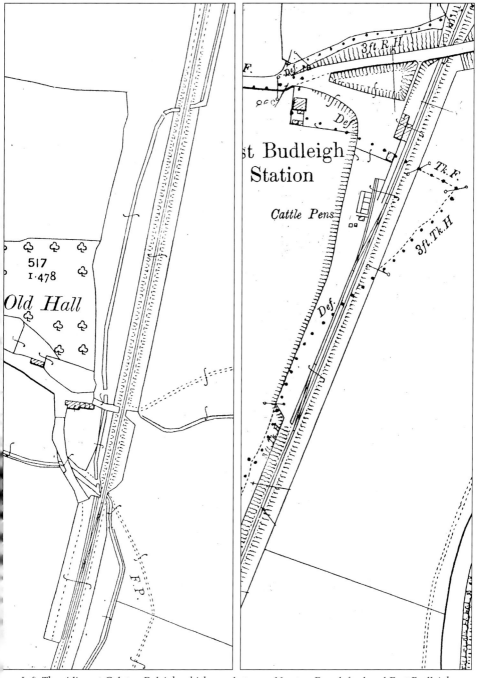

Left: The siding at Colaton Raleigh which was between Newton Poppleford and East Budleigh stations. *Reproduced from the 25", 1903 Ordnance Survey Map*

Right: East Budleigh station. *Reproduced from the 25", 1905 Ordnance Survey Map*

East Budleigh looking 'up'; the goods shed is on the left. The sign below the station name board reads 'For Otterton and Ladram Bay'. Notice that space has been left to allow for track doubling; 19th August, 1966.   *John H. Meredith*

Another view of East Budleigh, looking towards Newton Poppleford.   *Lens of Sutton*

This traffic ran almost up to closure to goods on 27th January, 1964. The southernmost spur accommodated camping coaches, and when Nos. S34 and S35 were noted in 1961, this had become an isolated length of track to avoid risk of damage by freight wagons using its only siding. This was slewed to connect by the local Engineer's Department permanent way men bi-annually for the trip to and from the coaches' winter quarters at Eastleigh.

East Budleigh was originally staffed by a station master and parcel porter: the former was withdrawn in the 1950s and its Grade 1 porter placed under Budleigh Salterton. On 25th April, 1966 the station was unstaffed. The guard of the last train of the evening was required to turn out the oil lamp. On one occasion the guard gave the driver the green light before turning out the lamp and, after turning it off, found to his dismay that the train had accelerated beyond reach. On arriving at Budleigh Salterton the staff were horrified to find the guard's door open and no guard to be seen. The thought immediately sprang to mind that he must have fallen out. They proceeded along the track looking for him and were greatly relieved to find him pounding towards them.

East Budleigh displayed a white-washed pebble message: 'for Ladram Bay' - a local beach and camping centre, because after World War II, quite an amount of camping gear came to the station for Scouts and Boys' Brigade camping at the bay. A 2.35 pm special ran from Exmouth on a few summer Saturdays during the late 1950s and early 1960s, conveying Scout parties returning to Waterloo. It called at most stations on the Budleigh branch and some on the main line.

Near East Budleigh station is Bicton Gardens, part of the Rolle Estate. One of its features is a delightful 18-inch-gauge railway, its signalling equipment originating from Lympstone station on the Exmouth branch.

The gradient continued to fall at 1 in 413, was level and then climbed at 1 in 388, followed by about 660 yds at 1 in 100 and almost three-quarters of a mile at 1 in 50, levelling out on the approach to Budleigh Salterton, (170 m. 58 ch.). Salterton, as it was called until 27th April, 1898, was originally a one-road station built of brick at a cost of £350 by J.C. Palmer, a local builder who also constructed East Budleigh station. The signal box was at the end of the 316 ft-long platform. When the extension to Exmouth was opened, a second, or up, platform of a similar length was added together with a small waiting shelter, the platforms being linked by a footbridge. The crossing loop held 17 wagons. The opening of the extension to Exmouth caused the eventual closure of the engine shed, as branch locomotives could then be stabled at Exmouth.

One special feature of the station from 1953 onwards, was the whitewashed pebbles spelling out a message, the actual wording being changed each year. That for 1959 was: 'A spot of glorious Devon, Budleigh Salterton'. The station won 15 first prizes in the Best Kept Station competition. Many first class passengers were booked as a considerable number of retired Servicemen lived in the town. Daily, the cash takings were placed in a bag which was put through the lid of a box chained to the handbrake column of a passenger train guard's van and taken to Exeter via Exmouth. Wages came from Exeter in a cash box to which the station master held a key.

In 1921 the staff consisted of a station master, clerk, signalman, checker, two porters and a porter-signalman. Thirty years later traffic required a station

A good view of the road bridge at the eastern end of Budleigh Salterton station. A well cleaned BR Standard class '3MT' 2-6-2T No. 82025 runs round its train, 9th July, 1959. *R.C. Riley*

Another view of No. 82025 now waiting to leave Budleigh Salterton with a train for Sidmouth on 9th July, 1959. Although the platform on the left does not allow much space, the station staff have been able to make some narrow flower beds to enhance the environment. *R.C. Riley*

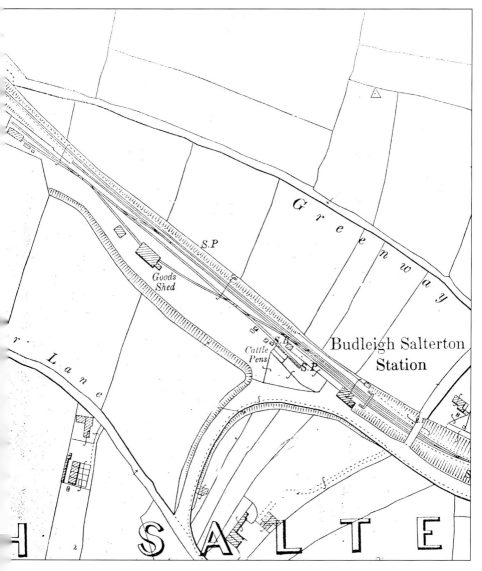

Budleigh Salterton station.   *Reproduced from the 25", 1905 Ordnance Survey Map*

Budleigh Salterton seen on 7th January, 1967, just before closure, looking towards Tipton St John's.   *E.Wilmshurst*

A close-up of the footbridge (No. 25A) at Budleigh Salterton, looking 'down'. The signal box can be seen at the end of the platform, with the goods shed beyond.   *Lens of Sutton*

master, two signalmen, a leading porter-signalman, leading porter, road motor driver and a summer clerk to assist with office work and ticket collecting. In 1962 two Class 4 signalmen worked from 6.25 am to 1.25 pm and 3.45 pm to 10.45 pm respectively; these men, in addition to their signalling duties, assisted with the loading and unloading of vans and labelling luggage, the leading porter-signalman manning the box from 1.25 pm to 2.40 pm. There was also a leading porter and a booking clerk. On summer Sundays one signalman was responsible for all station duties between 10.30 am and 8.40 pm. Budleigh's last station master was made redundant in October 1965 after holding the post for almost 20 years. The full complement of staff in 1966 should have been a clerk, two signalmen and a porter, but for some time the station just had one clerk, a signalman doing overtime and the assistance of a relief man.

One summer *c*. 1920, a non-stop Saturdays-only train ran through the station, a porter catching the tablet while the signalman stationed himself about 20 yds further along to hand over the tablet for the section ahead.

The sizeable goods yard with brick goods shed and a cattle dock was on the down side of the line. The station was closed to goods from 27th January, 1964. It dealt with coal for the gas works, one wagon daily of general goods from Nine Elms and after Budleigh Salterton market which was held on alternate Mondays, 20 to 25 cattle trucks had to be loaded. About 1919, during the herring season, as many as four vans of fish for Billingsgate Market would be attached to an afternoon passenger train, and, on one occasion, when a glut of herrings outstripped the number of available barrels, the surplus fish were loaded loose into a truck. From 1939 onwards, Hooker & Son sent shellfish in fish kits (small barrels) by passenger train. The fish came by rail from Kingsbridge in large barrels, and were sorted and dispatched in kits. A weekly consignment of cowhide was sent from the local slaughterhouses to tanneries 'in the raw', merely being rolled up and tied with strong cord. Prior to 1939, big moon daisies grew on the up side at Budleigh station and the staff picked them and made bundles which were despatched to Waterloo for distribution to London hospitals.

In the 1950s up to 40,000 tons of stone containing silica was sent away annually. This came by lorry from Black Hill Stone Quarries and was loaded on wagons at the station to be taken to Albright & Wilson, Portishead. Ordinary coal wagons were used for this traffic after being brushed out. Their use was economical as they would otherwise have been returned empty to South Wales.

Initially three trains ran from Budleigh daily - morning, afternoon and evening between service trains - and at Exmouth were combined into one train scheduled to leave at 10.10 pm. Because of the steep gradients between Budleigh and Exmouth, stone trains had to be limited to five or six wagons, and it was found more economical to work them to Exeter (from where they were forwarded by ordinary services) via Sidmouth Junction, though for a short period, both routes were used. Stone trains travelling via Sidmouth Junction were usually hauled by either a 'Woolworth', (an 'N' class 2-6-0), or a BR Standard class '3MT' 2-6-2 tank engine. The number of trains varied according to the quarry's requirements, but averaged about three a week. Following closure of the branch, quarry lorries conveyed the stone to wagons at Whimple

The waiting shelter on the up platform at Budleigh Salterton, 26th September, 1966. *A.E. West*

'0415' class 4-4-2T No. 82 stands at Littleham, with an Exmouth train, *c.* 1905.

Author's Collection

Littleham, looking towards towards Exmouth, pre-1959. Camping coaches are stabled on the left; wooden goods shed beyond, latterly used as a coal shed. *Lens of Sutton*

A close view of the signal box and level crossing at the Exmouth end of Littleham station. *Lens of Sutton*

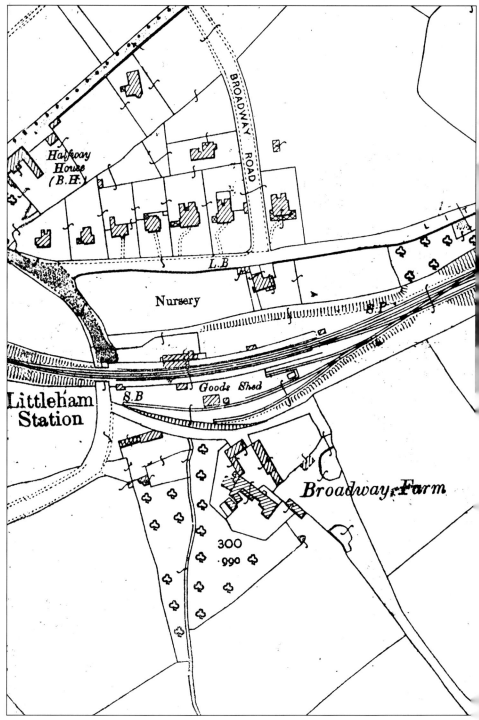

Littleham station.   *Reproduced from the 25″, 1905 Ordnance Survey Map*

station on the Exeter to Salisbury line.

In 1919 the single needle telegraph was still in use at Budleigh. In the interests of brevity, code words were used, two being 'Gum' and 'Falcon', the first meaning 'Referring to your communication of today' and the second 'No trace'. One day the junior porter was standing on the platform talking to a clergyman when the signalman having received a telegraph message from Tipton St John's box, came out from his cabin and called to the clerk to enquire if an article of lost property had been handed out from the previous down train. The clerk, busy dealing with parcels on the platform, shouted back, 'Give the b . . . . . s the Gum Falcon', whereupon the clergyman remarked, 'I understand the first part, but what does he mean by"Gum Falcon"?'

A large brass handbell was provided in the signal box, the original purpose of which was to warn staff and passengers that a train was on its way, but by 1919 its use for this had been discontinued, it being only employed to announce the ten o'clock time signal as it came over the telegraph instrument. Practice was for Queen Street to repeat the word 'time' on the telegraph and then at 10.00 am to relay the word 'ten' on receipt from Waterloo. The garden of a retired sea captain terminated at the lineside and whatever the weather, the old chap could be seen by the fence with watch in hand, waiting for the time signal.

Whenever a honeymoon couple travelled by train, and in 1919 there was little alternative, half a dozen detonators would be placed on the rail to give the newly-weds a good send-off. Traffic about this date was sometimes so heavy that the branch train conveying coaches from the 11.00 am from Waterloo could be held at Budleigh for up to 15 minutes in order that the vast quantity of luggage could be unloaded. The station site is now part of Norman's Superstores Limited, the goods shed being embraced in the building.

Beyond Budleigh Salterton the branch climbed on a gradient of 1 in 50 for 1½ miles, crossing a 54 ft high brick arch over Dalditch Lane. This was the highest single span in the county. After passing through the deep and impressive Knowle Cutting marking the summit of the line, trains descended for ¾ mile at 1 in 50, the gradient easing before approaching Littleham, (173 m. 71 ch.), on the level.

Littleham had a passing loop holding 26 wagons. Both platforms were 402 feet in length, a substandal brick-built station building with awning being, located on the up side, while on the down platform was a small timber waiting shelter, the signal box being placed at the Exmouth end controlling the crossing gates. In later years when the station was only staffed by a signalman, to avoid him crossing over to the ticket office on the up platform for ticket sales, a matching wooden extension for this purpose was added to the signal box in May 1961. Following local post-war housing development it was not unusual for 20 women, some with prams, to be waiting for a train to Exmouth, while during the summer season a fair amount of traffic was destined for the Sandy Bay holiday caravan camp situated a mile beyond the nearby village. On the down side there was a timber-built goods shed in the yard which had coal staithes, a cattle loading dock, four sidings and a shunting spur. One of the sidings was lifted some time prior to 1954. The station was closed to goods traffic on 27th January, 1964. The spur was used for stabling stock of the

Exmouth viaduct, looking east immediately after completion of the line in 1903.

Exmouth Library

Palms and shrubs make Exmouth station more attractive in this picture dated 30th May, 1936.

S.W. Baker

Cleethorpes-Exmouth train, as it arrived one Saturday and was required to be kept until it returned the following week, there being no spare stabling accommodation at Exmouth. Between two and four camping coaches were kept in the yard at Littleham. At the end of the 1964 summer season, camping coaches were discontinued on the Western Region and early the following January the Pullman Holiday Coaches at Exton (2), Littleham (2) and Camping Coaches at East Budleigh (2) and Newton Poppleford (2), were taken to Exmouth. In July they were moved to Exmouth Junction awaiting disposal in 1966, thus ending a popular feature begun in the 1930s.

Littleham was originally a country station serving an agricultural area, but latterly has been part of Exmouth. In 1912 it had a staff consisting of station master, clerk, signalman, (who also assisted with the labelling and loading of luggage when not crossing trains), working alternate weeks with a porter-signalman who had bill posting and platform duties as a porter; a checker, with goods office duties, goods accounts, checking and invoicing; a Grade 2 porter responsible for station cleaning including cattle pens and trucks, loading and unloading goods, shunting, sheeting and roping wagons. From the 1920s the staff was reduced to two signalmen and one Grade 1 porter under the supervision of the Budleigh station master. On Sundays one signalman carried out all the station duties.

Today all that remains of this former hive of activity is the red brick station house, now situated in Jarvis Close - the housing estate built on the station site.

From Littleham the line descended for 1¼ miles at 1 in 50, this gradient requiring lengthy through up trains on Saturdays to seek the assistance of a pilot engine. The line passed under the brick 3-arch bridge carrying the Salterton Road and wound down through the suburbs of Exmouth skirting Phear Park. Approaching the junction with the Exeter to Exmouth line, it crossed a major engineering feature, a curved 23-arch, 30 ft high brick-built viaduct some 352 yds in length, incorporating two girder bridges and wide enough for double track. It joined the line from Exeter at 175 m. 29 ch., immediately north of Exmouth signal box.

A 40 mph maximum speed restriction was imposed between Exmouth and Budleigh Salterton and 50 mph onwards to Tipton, with a 40 mph restriction through Newton Poppleford station. Electric token block posts were at Exmouth, Littleham, Budleigh Salterton and Tipton. Certainly as late as 1919, East Budleigh and Newton Poppleford having no signal box also had no single needle telegraph and were therefore completely cut off from the other stations, their only communication being by train.

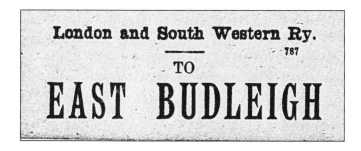

'M7' class 0-4-4T No. 253 arrives at Tipton St John's with a Sidmouth Junction to Exmouth train on 30th May, 1936. The timber-built office on the up platform has been removed since the previous photograph was taken, and the station name board on the left changed to the SR concrete pattern. *S.W. Baker*

'M7' class 0-4-4Ts Nos. 671 and 123 with the Budleigh Salterton and Exmouth portion of the 11.00 am ex-Waterloo near Shortwood Lane Bridge, west of Budleigh Salterton in 1938.
Fairlynch Museum

Chapter Eight

Train Services on the
Budleigh Salterton Branch

The first timetable on 15th May, 1897 gave eight trains each way on weekdays-only between Tipton St John's and Budleigh Salterton, one being a mixed train in addition to a separate goods working. With the extension to Exmouth in 1903, nine passenger trains and a goods train ran each way daily, the latter being limited to 15 loaded wagons between Exmouth and Budleigh Salterton. Some passenger trains had an extended stop at Budleigh Salterton.

In the summer of 1909 ten trains ran between Tipton and Exmouth with the addition of a short working train from Tipton to Budleigh Salterton and another from Budleigh Salterton to Exmouth. In the reverse direction there were 10 up trains, three having an extended stop at Budleigh Salterton, plus one between Exmouth and Budleigh Salterton. Three ran each way on Sundays between Exmouth and Budleigh Salterton. A time of 30 to 44 minutes was allowed for the journey of 11¼ miles, the time being generous as trains had to wait at Budleigh Salterton to cross. The weekday service in April 1910 was rather more liberal with eleven trains each way and an extra from Exmouth to Budleigh Salterton; however, no trains were run on Sundays in the winter half of the year. In July 1922 there were 10 trains plus three short workings (Exmouth-Budleigh) each way on weekdays only. The first Southern Railway timetable showed an improved service of 12 down and 11 up trains daily with no less than five short workings each way, but no Sunday trains. The winter service saw a slight reduction to 11 trains each way plus three short workings. In the summer of 1932 there were 13 trains each way on Mondays to Fridays, two of which were through to or from Sidmouth in each direction. On Saturdays there was an additional up train and, instead of through trains to Sidmouth, five up and eight down trains had coaches running to or from Sidmouth Junction. On summer Sundays, there were six each way, with one down train each from Sidmouth, Sidmouth Junction and Ottery St Mary. There was no winter Sunday service. In 1938 12 trains ran each way daily plus one short working to Budleigh Salterton and one from Sidmouth on Mondays to Fridays. On Saturdays there were 13 down and 14 up trains, while on Sundays, six ran each way. In 1948 nine down and eight up trains ran Mondays to Fridays, but one less each way on Mondays. There were eight trains each way on Saturdays and four on Sundays.

In the summer of 1951 10 trains were run each way and one more on Saturdays. Four trains ran in each direction on Sundays, all going through to or from Sidmouth. The Sunday service was withdrawn during the winter months, a practice which lasted until the line's closure. The 1955 service was nine down and eight up trains on Mondays to Fridays plus one each way on Fridays only, giving a service for branch passengers off the 6.00 pm Waterloo to Exeter express by changing at Sidmouth Junction and Tipton St John's. A train ran each way between Exmouth and Budleigh Salterton being formed on the outward journey with the rear portion of the 5.18 pm Exeter. By 1956 this

Swindon Cross Country unit arriving with the 5.18 pm Exmouth to Tipton St John's which became the 5.51 pm Tipton to Exmouth, 9th May, 1964. *Author*

BR Standard class '3MT' 2-6-2T No. 82010, shedded at Exmouth Junction, leaves East Budleigh with a down train. *Lens of Sutton*

	(From Sidmouth Junction)								
Ottery St. Mary Station	2 1,557	Up Platform	—	—	—	—	‧	—
Tipton St. John's Station .. .. (To Budleigh Salterton	2 224 6 763	Down side (Sidmouth side)	—	—	—	—	—	—
Sidmouth Station	3 24	Down side (Tipton St. John's end)	—	—	—	—	—	—

	(From Tipton St.John's)								
Budleigh Salterton Station	6 763	Down side (Exmouth end)	—	—	—	—	—	—
Littleham Station .. .. (To Exmouth ..	3 338 1 913	Down platform	—	—	Up loop	37 (Exmouth side)	Level

BETWEEN TIPTON ST. JOHN'S AND SIDMOUTH.

Loads of trains.—The maximum loads of trains worked by one engine between Tipton St. John's and Sidmouth stations are as follows :—

Down trains from Tipton St. John's to Sidmouth.	Up trains from Sidmouth to Tipton St. John's.
Passenger.—O.2 class T.1 class M.7 class engines, engines. engines. 128 tons 150 tons 160 tons Goods.—Not exceeding equal to 16 loaded goods wagons and 1 heavy van or 2 light vans. Mixed.—64 tons, equal to 6 loaded goods wagons, and one brake van.	Passenger.—O.2 class T.1 class M.7 class engines. engines. engines. 150 tons 170 tons 180 tons Goods.—Not exceeding equal to 23 loaded goods wagons and 1 heavy van or 2 light vans with a Guard in each. Mixed.—64 tons, equal to 6 loaded goods wagons, and one brake van.

A goods train run between Tipton St. John's and Sidmouth must have at the rear a heavy brake van of not less than 20 tons, which, whenever possible, should be a van fitted with sanding apparatus. Should, however, a brake van of this description not be obtainable, two smaller brake vans, with a man in each must be provided at the rear.

The Station Masters at Sidmouth Junction, Tipton St: John's and Sidmouth will be responsible for seeing that these instructions are obeyed.

Not more than one coach conveying passengers, or two horse boxes, P.L. vans, empty coaches, etc., may be attached outside the rear brake in either direction between Tipton St. John's and Sidmouth, and no vehicle must be so attached unless fitted with the vacuum brake complete.

SIDMOUTH.

Shunting.—When an empty coaching stock train is propelled by the engine from either of the platform lines to the single line in the direction of Tipton St. John's for the purpose of gravitating back into the station, it must be accompanied by the Guard (who must ride in the brake van nearest the engine) and a Shunter. The Shunter must not uncouple the engine until the train has come to rest on the single line and he has received an assurance from the Guard that the brake has been applied and the coaches are under control ; and the Guard must not allow the coaches to commence running back into the station until the engine has been shunted clear of the running line and the proper ground signal has been lowered for the movement to be made.

BETWEEN TIPTON ST. JOHN'S AND EXMOUTH.

Loads of trains.—The maximum load for one engine working a passenger train between Tipton St. John's and Exmouth is as follows :—

	O.2 class engines.	T.1 and M.7 class engines.
Down and up trains, between Tipton St. John's and Exmouth ..	140 tons	170 tons

The loads of goods trains between Exmouth and Budleigh Salterton must not exceed equal to 16 loaded goods wagons including heavy van (fitted with sanding apparatus).

East Budleigh.—Bogie coaches must not be shunted alongside the dock.

Budleigh Salterton.—Bogie coaches must not be shunted alongside the dock.

Littleham.—Bogie coaches must not be shunted alongside the dock.

Goods trains from the direction of Exmouth must not be brought to a stand at the Littleham up home signal.

Extracts from the Working Time Tables' Appendices 1934.

SEATON BRANCH.

Distance.		WEEKDAYS			Q Mxd. A			Distance.		WEEKDAYS			Q Mxd. A	
m.	c.			a.m.	p.m.		m.	c.			a.m.	p.m.	
—	—	Seaton Jc. .... ⊕ dep.	6 50	1 53	...	—	—	Seaton .... ⊕ dep.	5 30	3 48	...
1	49	Colyton .... { arr.	6 56	1 58	...	1	55	Colyton .... { arr.	5 36		...
		dep.	7 10	2 5½	...			dep.	5 40	3 53	
2	41	Colyford .... { arr.	7 14	2 6	...	2	47	Colyton .... { arr.	5 44	3 57	...
		dep.	7 18	2 9½	...			dep.	6 4	4 2	...
4	16	Seaton .... ⊕ arr.	7 24	2 14	...	4	16	Seaton Jc. .... ⊕ arr.	6 10	4 6	...

A—Not available on Saturdays 23rd June to 22nd September.

EXMOUTH JUNCTION SIDINGS, AND SIDMOUTH JUNCTION (VIA EXMOUTH) AND SIDMOUTH BRANCHES.

Distance from Exmouth Jc.		WEEKDAYS.							Q				SO				SO	
			arr. a.m.	dep. a.m.	arr. a.m.	dep. a.m.	arr. a.m.	dep. a.m.	arr. a.m.	dep. a.m.	arr. a.m.	dep. a.m.		arr. p.m.	dep. p.m.	arr. p.m.	dep. p.m.
m.	c.													To Exmouth Jc. Sdgs.				
—	—	Exmouth Jo. Sdgs. ...		6 5			9 2			10 15	Will not				...	...	...	...
2	69	Exmouth Jc. ...	6 6	6 12	9 3	9 9	9 9	9 40	10 17	10 21	run on Saturdays	Until			...	...	...
4	27	Newcourt Siding ...	...	...	9 17	9 40	10 29	(11.27)			23rd June	22nd Sept.			...	...	...
5	68	Topsham . . . . ⊕		6 20	9 46	10 17					to	only.			...	...	...
7	30	Woodbury Rd.			10-22	10 26					22nd Sept.				...	...	...
9	35	Lympstone . . . . ⊕		6 27	10 32	10 39									...	...	...
		Exmouth...... ⊕	6 32	...	10 45										...	...	...
11	9	Exmouth......... ⊕	...	...	...	...	arr. a.m.	dep. a.m.		11 10		11 35		Will not		Until	
14	25	Littleham . . . . ⊕	...	...	...	...	11 15	11 30	11 15	11 30	11 40	11 59		run on		22nd Sept.	
16	36	Budleigh Salterton ⊕	...	...	...	...			11 40	12 30	12 9	12 42		Saturdays		only.	
—	—	East Budleigh ⊕					Will not		12 35	12 45	12 47	12 57		23rd June			
19	38	Colaton Raleigh Sdg.	...	...	...	...	run on		12 49	12 54	1 1	1 6		to			
20	60	Newton Poppleford ⊕					Saturdays		12 58	1 7	1 10	1 17		22nd Sept.			
	m. c.	Tipton St. Johns ..⊕					23rd June		1 12	...	1 22						
	8 16	Sidmouth . ⊤					to								3 10		3 55
22	71	Ottery St. Mary . ⊤	...	...	...	...	22nd Sept.				1 58	1 50		3 22	3 40	4 7	4 14
25	68	Sidmouth Jct. ⊤	...	...	...	...	(10 19)	10 50				2 32		3 48	4 13	4 21	
							11 2				2 45	...		4 26	5 20	4 33	5 20

Distance from Sidmouth Jc.		WEEKDAYS.						Q Mixed. A		SO		SX		SO	
			arr. a.m.	dep. a.m.	arr. a.m.	dep. a.m.	arr. a.m.	dep. a.m.	arr. p.m.	dep. p.m.	arr. p.m.	dep. p.m.	arr. p.m.	dep. p.m.
m.	c.														
—	—	Sidmouth Jc. ......⊤	(6 35)	7 45		10 10							...	...
2	77	Ottery St. Mary . ⊤		7 54	10 19	(10 50)							...	...
5	08	Tipton St. Johns . ⊤	8 0	8 55				10 41					...	...
	m. c.	Tipton St. Johns ..⊕	9 10				10 56						...	...
	3 16	Sidmouth . ⊤			Will not								Until	
6	30	Newton Poppleford ⊕			run on				Commences				22nd Sept.	
9	32	East Budleigh ⊕			Saturdays				29th Sept.				only.	
11	43	Budleigh Salterton ⊕			23rd June									
14	59	Littleham ⊕			to									
16	33	Exmouth . . . . ⊕			22nd Sept.									
—	—	Exmouth......... ⊕	arr. a.m.	dep. a.m.						3 16		3 16		4 15
18	38	Lympstone . . . . ⊕							3 22	3 28	3 22	3 28	4 21	4 27
20	00	Woodbury Road ⊕							3 33	3 39	3 33	3 39	4 32	4 38
21	41	Topsham . . . ⊕							3 43	4 10	3 43	4 26	4 42	5 10
22	79	Newcourt Siding ...	(10 39)	11 37										
23	20	Digby's Siding . . .							4 32	4 47				
25	—	Exmouth Jc.	11 53	11 55					4 23	4 25	4 55	4 57	5 23	5 25
—	—	Exmouth Jc. Sdgs......	11 58						4 28		5 0		5 28	

A—When required on Saturdays 23rd June to 22nd Sept., start at 10.37 a.m. and arrive Sidmouth 10.52 a.m.

Extracts from the Working Time Tables' Appendices 1951.

working was extended to Tipton St John's, (with a corresponding down service being run), and the late Fridays service also ran on Saturdays. An additional service leaving Budleigh Salterton at 6.50 am was provided, the coaches being worked empty from Exmouth. Eleven trains ran each way on Saturdays and four on summer Sundays, with an additional through working from Honiton, (departure 1.42 pm) commencing on 30th June, 1957. In the autumn, the late Fridays and Saturday working ran throughout the week and subsequently an extra mid-morning and afternoon trip was introduced each way between Exmouth and Budleigh Salterton, chiefly to cater for residents on the new Littleham housing estate. From 1960 the new 5.45 pm express from Exeter to Budleigh Salterton returned to Exmouth as an additional passenger train and the 6.55 am from Budleigh Salterton ran through to Exeter.

The complete summer 1962 service was as follows:

Eleven down Mondays to Fridays plus four from Budleigh Salterton, two running through from Sidmouth.
Thirteen down Saturdays plus three from Budleigh Salterton, two running through from Sidmouth.
Five down on Sundays, one through from Honiton and two from Sidmouth.
Ten up on Mondays to Fridays plus three to Budleigh Salterton, two through to Sidmouth.
Twelve up on Saturdays plus one from Littleham, two running to Budleigh Salterton only. Two through to Sidmouth.
Four up on Sundays, two of which ran through to Sidmouth.

This pattern continued during 1963, although the morning and afternoon Budleigh trips were withdrawn at the end of the summer. On 4th November, 1963 two-car dmu suburban units appeared on nearly all of the services, but steam still remained on the 7.0 am Exmouth to Tipton and its return at 7.38, arriving at Exmouth at 8.4 am and continuing to Exeter as the 8.20 am 'fast'. Another steam hauled circuit was the 7.34 am from Exeter Central to Sidmouth, 9.31 am Sidmouth, 9.47 am Tipton and 11.28 am empty coaching stock Exmouth to Exeter. The 1.13 pm Tipton to Exmouth and its return at 1.42 pm also remained steam-hauled. This last working was unusual as only a single BCK coach (corridor brake composite) was booked, but this ultimately ceased on 25th January,1964 when the 9.53 am Mondays, Wednesdays and Fridays only freight from Exmouth Junction Sidings to Exmouth and thence 11.08 am to Tipton working was discontinued on 24th January. The 1.13pm Tipton passenger service was from then onwards worked by a single diesel power car.

Apart from the workings mentioned above and the 9.23 am dated summer Sundays Waterloo to Exmouth excursion, diesel locomotives began to take over the steam-hauled Saturdays-only through London trains during the summer of 1964.

A significant timetable alteration resulting from the introduction of the diesel scheme in November, was that the 7.20 pm Exmouth to Sidmouth and return at 8.30 pm terminated at Budleigh Salterton and returned at 8.00. The line then closed, except on Fridays when the 9.30 pm Exmouth to Tipton ran, retaining the service for branch passengers off the 6.00 pm Waterloo to Exeter. As this

A 3-car Swindon Cross Country dmu arrives at East Budleigh *en route* to Tipton St John's. A van can be seen in the goods siding. *Lens of Sutton*

Trains pass at Littleham. 'M7' class 0-4-4T No.30676 arrives with the 11.50 am from Exmouth. While '3MT' class 2-6-2T No. 82017 stands at the platform with the 11.32 from Tipton. Catch points are provided to guard against wrong line runaways down the incline and a board between No. 30676 and the level crossing gates warns of their presence. *H.B. Priestley*

express was relegated to a stopping service in the summer   timetable, the branch connection was thereafter provided off the 7.0 pm Waterloo to Exeter express on Fridays and summer Saturdays only, allowing for the first time an opportunity for Budleigh line passengers to return later from London.

Under dieselisation the summer 1964 service was basically unchanged except for some minor reductions, there being 10 down trains, (one through from Sidmouth, one through to Exeter), plus a late train on Fridays and two short workings. On summer Saturdays 10 plus two short workings operated. Five ran on Sundays, one from Honiton and the remainder from Sidmouth. In the up direction nine trains ran, (one through to Sidmouth and one from Exeter Central at 5.13 pm), plus the late Friday train and one short working to Budleigh Salterton which was the 5.45 pm 'fast' from Exeter Central. The 7.20 pm Exmouth, previously terminating at Budleigh Salterton, ran once again to Tipton for the summer only. Ten up trains ran on Saturdays, plus one from Littleham and one to Budleigh. Five ran on Sundays, four of which went to Sidmouth including one from Tiverton. The winter service saw a reduction of two trains each way, and of course, no Sunday service was run. Between January and June 1965 one through train ran each way between Exmouth and Sidmouth.

By the winter of 1964 steam deputized for the principal commuters' dmu 'express', the 5.45 pm Exeter Central to Budleigh Salterton, whenever that train, a through working from Ilfracombe was late. A switch of duty with the steam-hauled 5.49 pm 'stopper' from Exeter Central enabled the 'express' to run punctually. On arrival at Exmouth, two of the five WR coaches were detached to ease the load over the stiff gradient to Budleigh. This swan-song of steam finally disappeared when further diagram revisions were effected from 4th January, 1965.

In the timetable for June 1965 to April 1966 nine down trains plus the Fridays only service were shown, including one through to Exeter Central, four through from Sidmouth, and a further three short workings from Budleigh Salterton to Exmouth. Twelve down trains were run on summer Saturdays, including four from Sidmouth. On summer Sundays there were six down trains, five from Sidmouth, one going to Exeter Central. Eight trains ran in the up direction plus the 'Fridays only', one from Exeter Central and three through to Sidmouth. Two short workings ran to Budleigh Salterton, one of these from Exeter Central at 5.45 pm. Twelve up trains ran on summer Saturdays including four through to Sidmouth. Of the six up trains on summer Sundays, four ran to Sidmouth.

With the commencement of the summer 1966 timetable, through workings to and from Exeter via Exmouth ceased to operate, as the Budleigh Salterton service was made independent of Exmouth branch workings to facilitate the forthcoming closure at a date then unannounced. A reduced service of eight trains ran each way, with one short working at 8.15 am from Exmouth to Budleigh Salterton returning at 8.58. On Fridays and summer Saturdays, the branch connections still remained off the 7.0 pm Waterloo which had now been further decelerated as a result of the anticipated singling of the Salisbury to Exeter main line. The branch working involved a dmu leaving Exmouth at 10.5 pm for Tipton, returning at 11.15 to arrive Exmouth at 11.40 pm. On summer

The 11.8 am Exmouth to Tipton St John's freight hauled by 'M7' class 0-4-4T No. 30024, shunting at Littleham on 11th March, 1961. The first two vehicles are camping coaches, while another two are in the siding on the far left. *S.P. Derek*

BR Standard class '3MT' 2-6-2T No. 82010 on 18th June, 1960, berths the Eastern Region stock of the first Cleethorpes to Exmouth train at Littleham, to await return the following Saturday. *S.P. Derek*

Saturdays an augmented service ran with 10 trains each way, no short workings, but three starting from Sidmouth and one terminating there. After the summer Sunday service, similar to the previous year, the final weekday service of the winter consisted of seven each way, (three each serving Sidmouth and Sidmouth Junction), plus the short working and the late Friday service each way.

Main Line Through Services

Through coaches to and from Waterloo have been a feature from at least as early as 1914, while from 1927 on Fridays and Saturdays a train ran from Nottingham via Bath and the Somerset & Dorset Joint Railway, reaching the SR at Templecombe and travelling to Exmouth via Tipton St John's. In 1932 it left Nottingham at 9.50 am and arrived at 5.56 pm. On Saturdays an 11.10 am and 3.10 pm ran from Waterloo in addition to the train from Nottingham. In the up direction there was a 9.05 am to Nottingham and a 1.45 pm to Waterloo (on Fridays 22nd July to 9th September) and 9.22, 11.00 am and 2.00 pm to Waterloo and the Nottingham train on Saturdays.

From 19th July, 1926 when the 11.00 am ex-Waterloo for the West Of England was first named the 'Atlantic Coast Express' (ACE), the Sidmouth and Exmouth coaches were detached at Yeovil Junction. The Sidmouth coach ran non-stop Sidmouth Junction to Sidmouth, while the Exmouth portion stopped at all stations except Newton Poppleford. In the reverse direction, coaches were coupled to the up 'Atlantic Coast Express' at Yeovil Junction.

Normally there was one corridor brake composite coach for Sidmouth and another to Exmouth. With the winter timetable commencing 20th September, 1926, the 'ACE' stopped at Sidmouth Junction for Sidmouth and Exmouth coaches to be detached.

From the summer of 1928, the down 'ACE' stopped at Sidmouth Junction instead of Yeovil Junction. That year the up Plymouth and East Devon coaches ran as a separate untitled train. From 1930 onwards the 'ACE' departed from Waterloo at 10.35 am and ceased to serve East Devon, this being accommodated by the 11.00 am ex-Waterloo. In the summer of 1938 through services Waterloo to Exmouth via Budleigh Salterton were:

Down:
11.00 am, 3.00 pm Waterloo Mondays-Fridays.
8.47, 11.47 am, 3.00 pm Waterloo, 10.24 am Derby on Saturdays.
Up:
9.50 am, 12.01 pm Exmouth to Waterloo on Mondays to Fridays.
9.19, 10.38 am, 1.48 pm Exmouth-Waterloo plus 9.00 am Exmouth-Derby on Saturdays.
11.48 am Exmouth-Waterloo on Sundays.
Through trains usually only ran on Saturdays, at other times a through coach usually sufficed.

Suspended during World War II, the 'ACE' was restored on 6th October, 1947 leaving Waterloo at 10.50 am, arriving at Sidmouth Junction 2.8 pm, where the

Sidmouth and Exmouth coaches were detached. The following year through coaches from Waterloo left at 10.50 am Mondays to Fridays and 11.35 on Saturdays. In the up direction, departure was at 9.50 am and 9.10 am respectively, the former being attached to the 10.30 am from Exeter at Sidmouth Junction. In 1949 an additional through coach worked Mondays to Fridays at 11.50 am from Exmouth attached to the 12.30 pm from Exeter.

In 1950 the only changes to through services were departure from Waterloo at 11.00 am on Mondays to Fridays and 7.50 am on Saturdays.

From 1953 the Monday to Friday 11.50 am through Exmouth coach disappeared and Saturday trains left Waterloo at 8.05, 9.00 and 11.45 am, a pattern which was to last ten years. The 8.05 am from Waterloo was taken on to Exmouth from Tipton St John's by one of the two engines which had hauled it from Sidmouth Junction; the Exmouth portion of the second train had seven coaches and was double-headed through to Exmouth, while the eight coaches of the third train were also piloted. The 9.45 am Budleigh Salterton and 1.45 pm Exmouth to Waterloo were introduced in 1955, the former subsequently altered to return from Littleham. Both trains consisted of six coaches, the maximum load for one engine. Additionally a through train to Waterloo departed from Exmouth at around 9.25 am (exact times varied each year). This was normally an eleven coach maximum load for a double-headed working, usually timetabled to run 'fast' to Tipton St John's. On Christmas Eve 1958, there was an additional set of through coaches from Waterloo to Exmouth at 6.06 pm, a regular event on an evening prior to a Bank Holiday weekend. On 11th September, 1961 the 'ACE' was speeded to arrive Sidmouth Junction at 1.42 pm, five minutes earlier, with a corresponding earlier arrival for the through coaches at the respective branch terminii.

The high water mark of through services came in 1960-2 with the addition of the Saturdays-only, July-September 7.00 am Cleethorpes to Sidmouth and Exmouth and the 10.42 am Exmouth/11.07 am Sidmouth return working. It ceased running from September 1962 as a result of the S&D line being no longer used by through trains.

With the introduction of diesel multiple units in September 1963, through coaches on Mondays to Fridays were withdrawn. In the summer of 1964 the 11.45 am Waterloo was diverted to Ilfracombe and the up Sidmouth (9.32) and Littleham (9.10) trains combined. The 1965 summer was the last season of through services on the Tipton-Exmouth line, the times being 8.00, 10.00 am and 12.00 noon Waterloo to Sidmouth and Exmouth and 09.00, 11.15 am and 2.13 pm Exmouth and Sidmouth to Waterloo.

London and South Western Ry.

781

FROM WATERLOO TO

LITTLEHAM

Via EXMOUTH.

Chapter Nine

Locomotives and Coaches
on the Budleigh Salterton Branch

Locomotives appearing on the branch were much the same as those covered in the Sidmouth Junction to Sidmouth section. Beattie '329' class 2-4-0 well tank No. 253 was recorded working one of the first trains to Budleigh Salterton, while in 1903 Beyer, Peacock Double Framed 0-6-0 goods engines Nos. 0277/87, shedded at Exmouth Junction, worked the 8.10 am goods reaching Exmouth at 10.20 am and leaving for Tipton St John's at 10.45, picking up and setting down at intermediate stations. At Tipton, wagons left by the 10.00 am Sidmouth Junction to Sidmouth were collected and at 1.07 pm the goods returned to Exmouth, calling at each siding *en route*. Following its arrival at Exmouth at 2.52 pm, it proceeded to Exeter.

'N' class 2-6-0s appeared on stone trains from Budleigh Salterton, while 'West Country' class 4-6-2 No. 21C114 *Budleigh Salterton* and No. 21C115 *Exmouth* were ceremonially named at their respective towns on 26th June, 1946. The locomotives travelled via Tipton to avoid the restriction over the Clyst Viaduct on the Exmouth branch. O.V. Bulleid who designed the 'West Country' class was an Exmothian.

An unusual visitor on 7th February, 1947 was 'M7' class 0-4-4T No. 23 from Barnstaple shed. She was in pre-war Maunsell livery with large numbers on the tank sides.

The maximum load for one engine working a passenger train over the Budleigh Salterton line was:

BR class '3MT'	2-6-2T	200 tons
LM class '2'	2-6-2T	170 tons
'M7' class	0-4-4T	170 tons
'02' class	0-4-4T	140 tons

The headcodes used on the branch were a diamond on the near-side mid-iron, and a disc on the off-side mid-iron from 1st May, 1901; after 1905 it was a disc at the centre of the buffer beam.

A small single road shed erected at the west end of Budleigh Salterton yard, was used by the tank engine when the branch opened in May 1897. Built of timber, the shed measured 50 ft by 18 ft. Outside was a coal stage and water tank. When the line was extended to Exmouth in 1903 it was still retained to service locomotives working trains terminating and commencing at Budleigh Salterton. Timetable alterations abolished such workings and the shed became redundant and was demolished in 1925, though its sidings were not taken out of use until 2nd February, 1965.

The first locomotive shed at Exmouth was a one-road, single-ended building of timber, with a 42 ft diameter turntable outside. This latter feature was removed before building on the same site, in the late 1920s, a new shed from concrete blocks at a cost of £2,200. As with its predecessor, an outside wall

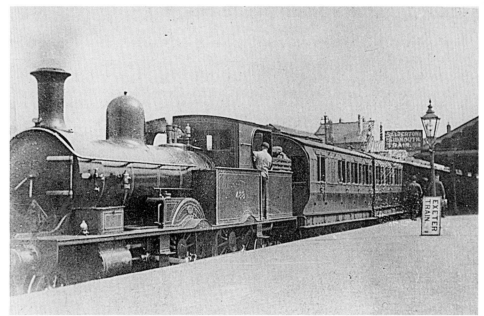

'0415' class 4-4-2T No. 488 stands at Exmouth, c. 1905. The notice on the lamp post indicates 'Salterton & Sidmouth Train'.

Author's Collection

Trains crossing at Littleham, 30th May, 1936; 'M7' class 0-4-4T No. 376 heads the up train.

S.W. Baker

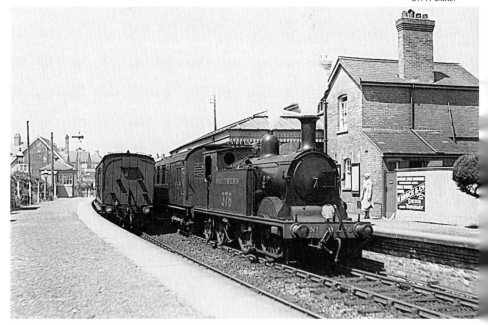

faced the passenger platforms and was covered with advertisements.

Exmouth locomotive depot was a sub-shed of Exmouth Junction, its locomotives bearing the BR shed code 72A. There were eight pairs of men at the depot in its heyday, three cleaners and four locomotives. The driver in charge of the depot always worked the middle shift. Exmouth-based engines faced Sidmouth Junction, while Sidmouth-based engines faced towards Sidmouth. In 1960 Exmouth shed had an allocation of four engines, though individually they varied from day to day.

Latterly stock generally consisted of two class '3' 2-6-2Ts, one class '2' 2-6-2T and an 'M7' 0-4-4T. As there were no coaling facilities, each engine visited Exmouth Junction daily for this purpose and also necessary examination. A coal wagon was kept at Exmouth for topping-up purposes. Following the closure of Exmouth locomotive shed on 4th November, 1963, the date from which most trains were diesel-operated, the building was demolished in the summer of 1967.

On the Budleigh Salterton branch the Waterloo through services were usually composed of the latest main line corridor stock applicable to the period, occasionally affording on one train contrasting standards of accommodation as observed in August 1959 when the 9.52 am Exmouth to Tipton St John's consisted of a Bulleid corridor 2-set (for Waterloo), an ex-LSWR 10 compartment second and a Maunsell corridor 2-set. 'Atlantic Coast Express' coach roof-boards sometimes adorned the through portion of the corresponding down service. The Cleethorpes to Exmouth train was composed of either all Eastern Region, or all Southern Region stock on alternate weeks. Trains of seven to eleven corridor coaches were double-headed on the branch section, while between Exmouth and Tipton, (and vice versa), certain passenger trains not exceeding three coaches, could be worked without a guard.

With the exception of the through trains between Budleigh and Exeter using the newer BR Standard compartment 3-sets, most Budleigh Salterton branch services from about 1959-60 were formed with Maunsell corridor 2-sets. These comprised a brake composite, with either a brake second, corridor second, or open second, coach built between 1930-6 and which for many years had been used on secondary duties after their displacement from main line duties. WR maroon stock was used on the remaining local steam-hauled working in the spring of 1964, when the 7.0 am Exmouth to Tipton St John's was hauled by a BR class '4MT' 2-6-4T.

London and South Western Ry.
787
TO
BUDLEIGH SALTERTON

Appendix

Station Statistics

	Sidmouth Junction			Ottery St Mary			Tipton St John's			Sidmouth		
	1928	1932	1936	1928	1932	1936	1928	1932	1936	1928	1932	1936
No. of passenger tickets issued	21,015	15,783	13,373	20,190	11,509	9,601	10,524	5,847	5,014	30,253	16,368	14,916
No. of tickets collected	22,489	17,414	16,061	29,027	16,283	17,360	10,480	6,328	6,157	57,432	35,244	37,910
No. of season tickets issued	58	95	112	101	68	113	16	38	39	174	282	315
No. of platform tickets issued	1,354	520	325	908	152	43	-	-	-	8,235	6,628	6,952
Parcels forwarded	2,108	1,990	1,331	2,419	1,593	1,304	1,433	799	442	5,885	4,939	4,580
Parcels received	2,146	1,879	2,009	5,862	6,382	7,452	406	547	590	29,332	33,510	36,208
Horses forwarded	39	49	95	25	1	6	9	18	11	3	17	14
Horses received	67	42	102	12	5	3	7	15	10	5	14	4
Milk forwarded (churns 1928, gallons 1932 & 1936)	13,050	116,523	34,098	356	9,116	-	2,425	12,876	8,519	428	10	56
Milk received (churns 1928, gallons 1932 & 1936)	48	1,276	-	-	68	-	23	45	-	1,517	17,669	20,138
General merchandise forwarded (tons)	542	416	489	1,317	1,265	768	177	73	69	1,197	1,172	829
General merchandise received (tons)	3,250	1,637	1,914	4,398	4,771	5,089	1,033	1,051	851	6,982	5,751	6,209
Coal, coke, patent fuel, forwarded (tons)	-	6	5	-	7	-	-	-	-	30	11	71
Coal, coke, patent fuel, received (tons)	881	1,143	1,224	4,343	4,910	4,370	397	250	237	12,347	13,162	12,688
Other minerals, forwarded (tons)	128	192	74	1,248	330	60	-	-	100	216	190	466
Other minerals, received (tons)	1,898	343	75	2,064	1,038	345	100	34	7	5,107	123	332
Livestock forwarded (No. of trucks)	262	102	118	156	24	153	8	2	7	22	10	10
Livestock received (No. of trucks)	85	26	15	50	14	12	27	5	-	69	5	4

Station Statistics

	Newton Poppleford			East Budleigh			Budleigh Salterton			Littleham		
	1928	1932	1936	1928	1932	1936	1928	1932	1936	1928	1932	1936
No. of passenger tickets issued	7,856	5,336	4,306	12,993	3,049	2,170	37,088	15,237	12,424	14,453	4,119	3,109
No. of tickets collected	5,744	3,453	3,919	18,082	5,052	3,230	55,420	22,979	19,217	18,443	4,874	4,363
No. of season tickets issued	41	49	48	78	25	28	196	110	98	70	37	25
No. of platform tickets issued	-	-	-	30	13	3	4,483	3,435	1,818	160	13	2
Parcels forwarded	580	581	594	921	563	377	3,536	2,942	2,493	559	368	410
Parcels received	598	1,122	1,102	1,186	1,406	1,554	14,295	14,559	16,433	1,604	2,244	1,889
Horses forwarded	-	-	-	-	1	7	27	26	81	1	2	-
Horses received	-	-	-	2	2	7	12	29	70	1	2	-
Milk forwarded (churns 1928, gallons 1932 & 1936)	-	35	-	635	3,178	282	296	2,422	-	-	369	1,149
Milk received (churns 1928, gallons 1932 & 1936)	-	-	-	-	-	-	118	1,480	259	-	2,629	553
General merchandise forwarded (tons)	169	58	70	473	351	232	381	353	226	63	70	45
General merchandise received (tons)	873	714	728	1,100	868	515	1,840	1,942	1,291	483	348	349
Coal, coke, patent fuel, forwarded (tons)	-	-	-	-	-	10	-	11	-	12	-	-
Coal, coke, patent fuel, received (tons)	620	857	940	1,111	940	1,023	5,010	5,891	4,955	1,752	1,831	649
Other minerals, forwarded (tons)	-	-	-	-	-	-	38	90	62	537	36	-
Other minerals, received (tons)	297	159	45	1,650	75	15	1,994	1,271	273	2,141	109	94
Livestock forwarded (No. of trucks)	9	3	3	82	21	16	6	-	-	30	3	16
Livestock received (No. of trucks)	-	1	1	72	18	11	20	8	1	25	6	5

Notes: Camping coach at Newton Poppleford from 1935.
Budleigh Salterton platform ticket machine removed 1936.

Bibliography and Acknowledgements

History of the Southern Railway; R.M. Bonavia
Devon Harbours; V.C. Boyle & D. Payne
Locomotives of the LSWR; D.L. Bradley
Closed Stations & Goods Depots; C.R. Clinker
Exmouth Milestones; E.R. Delderfield
Railway Landmarks in Devon; J. Hall
London & South Western Engine Sheds: Western District; C. Hawkins & G. Reeve
Guide to Sidmouth; P.O. Hutchinson
History of Sidmouth; P.O. Hutchinson
Exe Valley Railway; J. Owen
Track Layout Diagrams of the Southern Railway & BR SR: Section 5; G.A. Pryer
A Story of Sidmouth; A. Sutton
A Regional History of the Railways of Great Britain: No. 1, the West Country; D. St John Thomas
The London & South Western Railway, Vols. 1 & 2; R.A. Williams
Southern Titled Trains; D.W. Winkworth
Newspapers: *Exeter Flying Post*; *Exeter Evening Post*; *Express & Echo*; *Exmouth Chronicle*; *Exmouth Journal*; *Sidmouth Herald*; *Western Morning News*
Magazines: *Engineering*; *Railway Magazine*; *Trains Illustrated*
Various Acts of Parliament

Grateful acknowledgements for assistance is due to: M.J.B. Blackstone; W.G. Clarke; L.L.G. Dolling; Miss J. Gawne, Fairlynch Arts Centre & Museum, Budleigh Salterton; the staff of Exmouth Library; Dr G. Gibbens, The Museum, Sidmouth; W.H. Hoare; S. Murch; R.E. Perkins, Sidmouth District Ratepayers' Association; G.T. Reardon; D.R. Steggles and R.J. Vince.

Special thanks go to S.P. Derek who very kindly made his notes available and checked and supplemented the manuscript, and also the late P.K. Tunks who gave great assistance with timetable information.

Gosford Gates level crossing - the former gate on the down side, now used for entrance to a field, is seen here on 18th July, 1989.   *Author*